welcome

What sounds more scrumptious: brownies a la mode or a mountain of vanilla ice cream atop a warm, chewy, delectable brownie? How would you prefer someone to describe your home: a small house or a quaint dwelling? A big house or a spacious abode? How about this one – would you rather slip into a red dress or a silky, scarlet gown? Chances are you'd choose the latter descriptions. The difference? **It's all in the words.**

Words are powerful.

They can express feelings, add insight and bring understanding to everyday situations.

The same holds true with our works of art. The words used add meaning and provide more understanding. By using the perfect words, we can better convey the emotion of a photo or an experience.

In *Designing with Words*, we've gone beyond the depths of the dictionary and the throes of the thesaurus to use words in ways we never thought possible, from the obvious to the sublime. Don't be intimidated – this isn't a journaling idea book. Rather, we show you creative, distinctive and effective ways to incorporate words not only on scrapbook pages but on all types of projects, from candles and cards to altered clocks and books. And the techniques aren't project-specific...if you see a technique used on scrapbook page, go ahead and try the same thing on a wall hanging or an altered tin. No matter the project, the words you choose, together with your personal journaling, can express heartfelt sentiments and turn an average project into a spectacular creative quest.

Enjoy your tour through this artistic lexicon and start using words to expand your creative vocabulary and enrich your "words of art."

chapter one
background noise

Imagine watching your favorite movie without any sound. Would it be as scary, as romantic, as happy or as peaceful? Background music and sound set the mood and make what you're viewing complete. The same is true for your scrapbook pages — they become complete with the words you use. Consider using words as a background to enhance the feel of your project and let the words become your soundtrack.

Rubber stamp words with VersaMark ink on a dark shade of cardstock. Heat emboss with clear embossing powder. To make the words stand out, rub them generously with various colors of metallic rub-ons, then polish with a paper towel. For the title piece, follow the same steps, but start with light green cardstock and use a black pigment ink. **Idea to note:** The journaling is hidden behind the hinged photo. Simply cut the photo into two pieces and add a hinge to each piece.

Blessing
BY JENNIFER

DESIGNING *with* words

Inspiration and ideas for adding meaning to your scrapbooks, cards and gifts through the power of words.

featuring

Jennifer Ditz McGuire
Renee Camacho
Debbie Crouse • Carol Wingert
Kristina Nicolai-White
Tracy Robison
Lisa Russo • Janelle Smith

table of Contents

School Book
BY TRACY

Design the text to print on one 12" x 12" piece of cardstock, which will be cut and pieced to create the accordion-fold book. To create the background text, make a text box that covers the entire page. Fill with words and phrases in a small font. Create text boxes using larger fonts and layer over the small text. Print the sheet and slice into thirds horizontally. Score each strip every 3 1/2". When folded, you should have three 3 1/2" blocks with about 1 1/2" to overlap when you attach the strips together. Tracy made one of the blocks for her cover, cutting it from the end of one of the strips. Attach the three strips together at the overlaps with double-sided tape to make the concertina strip. Cut a front and back cover from chipboard. Stamp the mat board with metal stamps and attach the front block to the cover. Attach the front and back covers to the book and tie with a ribbon closure.

Climb
BY RENEE

Print title and descriptive words on the background cardstock. Cut slits in various places in the background paper using an X-Acto knife. Slide cardstock, patterned papers and photos in the slits.

Spirit Words

Sometimes when I am creating a layout or piece, I find that doing old-fashioned journaling actually takes attention away from the emotion or feeling of the project. Instead, I find that I can better express myself using simple words. To do this, look at the photo and jot down whatever words first pop into your mind.

Then go to www.thesaurus.com and look up other words with the same meaning. Look for words that draw attention to, empower and add spirit to your piece. Use them as part of your background or embellishment. Together they will express the emotion you are aiming for. You will never be disappointed!

Jennifer

Adore Tag
BY JENNIFER

the process

Create a large tag from cardstock. Cut various textured and printed papers into 1" squares. Age some of the pieces with sandpaper, needles and brown ink. Adhere to the tag and stamp various words over the background. Add photo, tag and fibers.

Walter & Erna Zehnder
···1929···
Married 73 Years

the process

Duets
BY KRISTINA

Write lyrics on a transparency with a thin Sharpie marker. Layer strips of patterned papers to create a customized background. Attach the transparency to the layout with eyelets. Rubber stamp large letters on a glossy transparency using a liquid ink, such as chalk ink. Lay vellum over the top and rub your fingers over the letters to transfer the image to the vellum. Stamp title to the front of the vellum. Ink a portion of a stamp for the square tag. Lay the stamp down—ink side up—and press the tag onto the stamp. This enables you to position the image on the tag.

Rugby
BY LISA

Paint watercolor paper with diluted walnut ink. Let dry. Print text in various fonts, then tear into a strip. Antique the edges with black ink. Adhere to page and secure with snaps. Tear pieces of patterned and black papers for a unique corner embellishment. Print the text to place behind the bookplate, then stipple with inks. Attach the bookplate with twine.

Nature

BY RENEE

*Using a masking medium as your ink,
rubber stamp images onto glossy paper.
Allow to dry.* Use a brayer to apply ink
onto the glossy paper. To create the mottled
look, spritz the brayer with water one
additional time and go over the entire page.
Stitch a strip of paper over the bottom of the
photo and tie a tag to the strip. **Idea to note:**
To add additional interest, sew along the vines
of the leaves with thread and rub with ink.

Wedding Day Bliss

BY RENEE

Attach all patterned papers to
a cardstock base. Crumple the
edges to create a worn look.
Dry emboss each letter onto
the back of the cardstock base
using a letter template. Turn
the layout over and place the
letter template on the top of
each dry-embossed letter and
wipe with an embossing pad.
Sprinkle with embossing
powder and heat emboss.

Studio
Bulletin Board
BY JENNIFER

Rubber stamp words onto a bulletin board with dye ink, making sure to press firmly. Lightly spray board with walnut ink for an aged look. Wrap board with rick rack and add embellishments.

Wedding Frame
BY JENNIFER

Computer print a bible verse in brown on light green cardstock and print the main, large words in very light gray. Trace the light-gray words with watercolors to make it look handwritten. Lightly stamp and sponge the entire page using pale ink colors. When complete, lightly mist the entire piece with walnut ink. Use a knife to scratch the borders of a photo, then rub with walnut ink. Adhere to the background and put in a frame. Tie ribbon around the frame and secure with a charm.

chapter two

MARK MY word

When a person is so sure of himself he's willing to have someone record his words, he might comment, "Mark my word." So when you're certain of what you want to say on a creative project, don't be timid. Mark your word and just to be sure, stamp it in ink! Use the creative ideas featured in this chapter to leave your mark on your masterpiece.

Chloe
BY RENEE

Rubber stamp an image and name using clear embossing ink, then heat emboss with clear embossing powder. Swipe ink over the patterned paper to accentuate the embossed letters and images. Use a calligraphy tip and walnut ink to add journaling

CHLOE

Chloe loves life. This spring she has enjoyed every little sound... every flower... every touch... & every new flower so many new things, so little time.

APR 2 0 2003

Separate an oversized piece of mica into three layers of similar thickness. Stamp images and words on each layer with StazOn ink. Printed transparencies could also be inserted at different levels. Adhere the layers together with Diamond Glaze. Using the direct-to-paper method, ink the slide mounts, then embellish with rubber stamps, photos, labels, etc. Encase the mica between the two slide-mount frames.

the process

Paris
BY CAROL

Heart
BY JENNIFER

Stamp the word "heart" with VersaMark ink and emboss with clear embossing powder. Next, heavily paint blue watercolor over the word, frequently dabbing off excess watercolor from embossed letters. Stamp the same quotation repeatedly on the background paper. Print remainder of title on transparency and adhere with liquid glue. Print journaling on transparency tag and tuck into layout.

Little Notes
BY JENNIFER

Cut little cards from glossy paper. Rubber stamp a message with resist ink. When dry, use a foam make-up applicator to swirl color from a chalk inkpad over the front of the card. Punch hole and add ribbon. Decorate the tin using the same technique.

the process

Camacho Stationery

BY RENEE

the process

Die cut a portfolio from chipboard. Cover the portfolio with patterned papers. Create note cards to fit inside the portfolio. Sew rings onto the portfolio and tie with ribbon to close. **Idea to note:** Use rubber-carving tools and soft carving rubber to create a personalized stamp. Simply trace or draw the image in reverse and carve it out. For an extra handmade touch, leave a few rough areas to give it a bit more character.

A Day in the Park

BY TRACY

Rubber stamp on labels while still on the sheet, overlapping the circles and adding the words. When dry, peel off and place on the background cardstock as shown. Stamp the large words in a circular fashion on the background. Ink the edges of the cardstock and sand the stickers, background paper and edges of the photos. Paint the stitched tin tile with acrylic paint and sand the edges when dry. Stamp with dye ink and attach to page.

the process

Finicky
BY JENNIFER

Cut letters from chipboard. Cover with white pigment ink and two layers of embossing enamel. While hot, sprinkle in clear glass beads. Add another layer of embossing enamel. Again, while hot, press in tissue paper that has been stamped with StazOn ink. Paint the tin with acrylic paint, then gently sand. Add words around the layout and stamp a message directly on twill.

the process

Sea and Sand
BY RENEE

Stencil letters in different sizes onto the background using VersaMark ink. Heat emboss to create raised and darker portions. Print photo on canvas for a muted look. Attach to page along with seashell accents. Cover entire page with vellum, tearing holes for the background to peek through. Create a resist title strip by placing negative portions of the stencil on cardstock and swiping the inkpad directly over the letters, smoothing in a circular motion to blend. Heat emboss the lower left corner of the layout. **Idea to note:** Create a "salt and pepper" look by sprinkling a bit of black powder into bottle of clear embossing powder before using.

the process

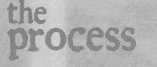

words of wisom

According to Webster (Mr. Definition himself!), a definition is the action or the power of describing, explaining or making definite and clear. So the significance of your project can become clearer by incorporating actual definitions. Notice how Tracy highlights definitions that describe Cliff by using a gold-leafing technique. And look how Renee draws attention to the word "wonder" using a bookplate filled with glaze. Try some of the same techniques and use definitions on your pages to clearly define the purpose of your project.

Fans
BY TRACY

Create definitions and title words using text boxes. Layer the boxes to achieve desired look. Print IN REVERSE on a laser printer (or make a photocopy from an ink jet print). Place on cardstock, image-side down. *Use* an image-transfer pen to transfer the words onto the cardstock. Make the title by inking cork rounds with red ink, then stamping with shadow letter stamps and black ink.

Sam
BY JENNIFER

the process

Create a definition to go with a photo. Print the definition on strips, wipe with VersaMark ink and heat emboss with embossing enamel. Frame the photo with the strips. Print some of the background definitions in light gray and cut other definitions from an old dictionary.

Laughter
BY TRACY

the process

Design the laughter definitions within a text box. Make the background a dark color and make the text white. Print on an ink jet transparency. Cut two circles from the transparency - one large and one small. Using Hermafix Permanent Transfer Dots, place random stripes on the background cardstock, checking to make sure gold will highlight words on the transparency after the leafing is complete. Rub gold leafing onto the dots and dust away any residue with a soft brush. Adhere the transparency circles over the gold leaf. Stamp the red cardstock with random images using ink of a similar tone. Cut out the title from red cardstock that has been stamped with a script stamp. Stamp brass label with permanent ink.

15

Defining...Comfort
BY CAROL

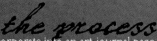

Scan and print definition pages in several sizes. Crop as necessary to incorporate into an art-journal page. For a special touch, cover a stencil letter with a portion of the definition and cut out the stencil areas.

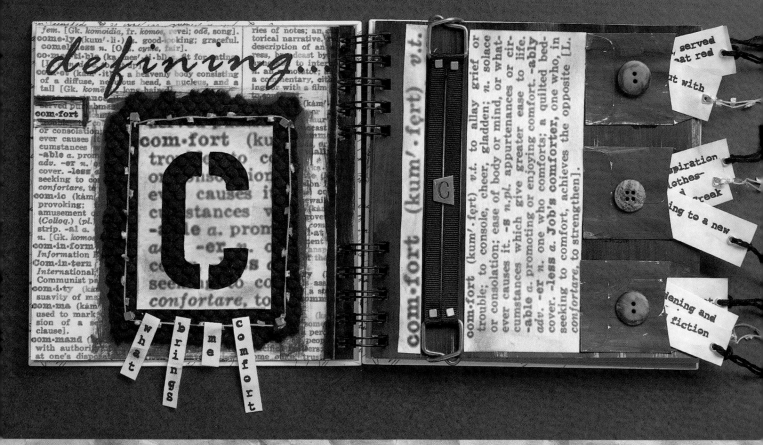

You Card
BY RENEE

Create a background of definitions. Print out title and trace onto a shrinky-dink, 50% larger than the intended size. Cut out and heat to shrink. Rubber stamp the rest of the title and heat emboss. String ribbon along the top for added color.

the process

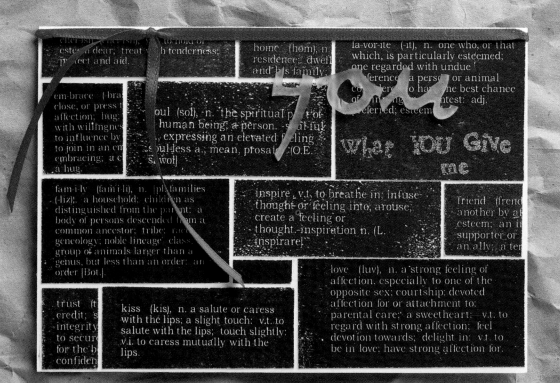

Wisdom
BY RENEE

Trim patterned paper to size, then antique the edges with brown ink. Attach to a brown cardstock base. Attach the dictionary page to the layout with eyelets. Highlight one of the definitions with a bookplate and fill with a clear glaze. Antique other definitions with walnut ink. Age alphabet letters with ink and attach with pop-dots.

Grow
BY RENEE

Trim patterned papers in horizontal strips and attach to a cardstock base. Drench ruler patterned paper two times in walnut ink to make the center strip. Antique the edges of the photo mat. Trim definitions into strips and use near the bottom as a border. Mount the main walnut-inked definition on patterned paper and mount with pop-dots. **Idea to note:** The journaling for the layout is included on a pull-out tag placed in an envelope.

spoken word

Philip G. Hamerton humorously quipped, "Have you ever observed that we pay much more attention to a wise passage when it is quoted, than when we read it in the original author?" Why do quotations have such an impact on people? Usually, they make us stop and think. Sometimes we have to reread a quotation to understand the meaning and get the full effect. So putting quotations on a scrapbook page—whether it's another's words or precious comments from children—is a great way to get people to pay more attention to your creations.

Synchronicity
BY KRISTINA

the process

Tear a manila folder to make the covers of the "Quotables" book. Embellish, then age with chalk ink. For the inside pages, tear off ends of manila tags, add quotations and insert between the covers. Clip together with a bulldog clip. Stamp images on the library card holder. Tie a tag to the bulldog clip and insert booklet into card holder. Attach to layout. Journal on torn and aged vellum. Stamp letters on a green strip, adhere the vellum to the back of the strip, then add to page.

Paint a wooden scrapbook with gesso. Adhere patterned papers to the front and back covers. Cover the insides, as well. Hand cut the title from brown cardstock stamped with a script rubber stamp. Tear random pages from an old dictionary and ink the edges with brown ink. Adhere to the front cover. Apply a white glue to the edges of the book and allow to get tacky. Use a brush to apply gold leafing. Attach tag and tile letters, and stamp butterfly images in brown ink. Design the inside pages using a variety of fonts and colors. Print on cream cardstock. Ink the photo corners with a sponge.

Words of Wisdom
BY TRACY

the process

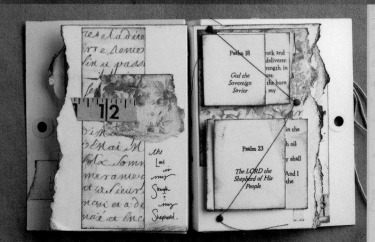

Book of Psalms
BY RENEE

Use two large square tags for the covers of the book. Score the covers with a bone folder so they open easily. Insert torn paper for filler pages. Punch holes along the spine of the book and bind with twine. Decorate the rest of the book as desired. Renee included several of her favorite Psalms inside. To view, unclasp the thread and unfold the paper.

the process

Excerpts
BY LISA

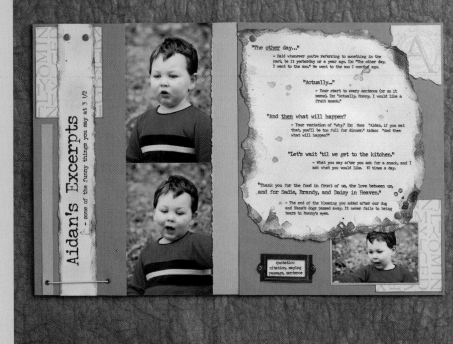

the process

For the left page, adhere a brown cardstock strip and a torn green strip to background using foam tape. Adhere photos under the edges of the strips. Print journaling and title. Tear, then use the lemon juice burning technique around the edges (see below). Stipple with dye inks to age. Secure with snaps and eyelets. For accents, stamp images with sand-colored ink, trim or tear, then edge with black ink.

LEMON JUICE BURNING

1. Lightly brush the edges of cardstock with lemon juice. Do not soak (blot if necessary).

2. Gently run a heat-embossing gun over the lemon juice. As the sugar in the juice caramelizes, it will turn golden brown. Let cool.

3. Re-heat the golden edges as desired. The more you heat, the darker the color.

4. For burnt "spots," drip the lemon juice, then blot immediately. Heat until you reach desired color.

Still talking – September 10, 1994

Get Married
BY LISA

To create the old-looking photo, scan a color photo, convert it to grayscale and add "grain" to make it grainy. Add an edge to the photo, then print on canvas paper.

the process

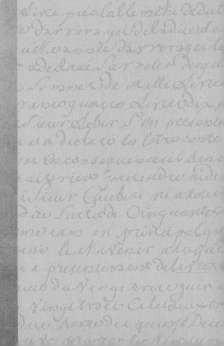

The Beauty of the Seasons
BY TRACY

Print or transfer text onto background cardstock. Design the photo "patches" and print onto transfer paper in reverse. Iron transfers onto calico and tear into patches. Sew a small button on each corner and mount on background.

the process

journaling...

A written conversation. That's what journaling is to me. It's not a formal writeup, a description of events, or a paragraph that's been tweaked into vanilla blandness.

When I sit down to journal, I first envision my audience - and it varies by piece. It might be my son, husband, mother, best friend, a legion of other mothers, or even myself. Then I talk to them. I pretend they're across the table from me, looking at my photos or completed layout, and I talk to them about it. I use written words to convey exactly what I would say. I'm a fairly sarcastic person, and it shows in my journaling. I think humor is key to drawing your audience in to your story. If they laugh, I've succeeded.

My hope is that someday the great-great grandchild I won't get to meet will browse through my books and say, "Wow, Grandma Russo was a sassy lady!" And they'll be right.

Lisa

Tile Coasters
BY JENNIFER

Drip several drops of two or three different ink colors onto a scrap piece of felt. Rub the inks over the surface of a white bathroom tile and let dry. Spray tile with a fixative. Meanwhile, create quotations on a computer. Tape a piece of white tissue paper onto a piece of cardstock. Set your printer to the ink transparency setting and print. Remove tissue from cardstock. You could also stamp words on the tissue with StazOn ink. *the process*

Using make-up applicators, apply a thin layer of Future Floor Polish over the tile. Lay printed tissue on the tile and carefully apply another layer of polish. Allow the tissue to wrinkle a little to give it a textured and aged look. Let dry and carefully cut off excess tissue. Apply three coats of shellac to protect the coaster. Finally, add small pieces of felt to the bottom of the tiles.

drop a line

The United States Postal Service delivers more than 200 billion letters per year. That's 2,300 pieces of mail per letter carrier per day! Once the letters are received, however, what happens to the letters and stamps? Most are thrown away. But instead of throwing them away, use them to embellish projects or as inspiration for your next creative endeavor. You can bet these projects won't be "returned to sender!"

Me, Defined
BY RENEE

Make a tag book by adhering the bottom portion of two tags together with linen hinging tape. Create the inside pages with various types of envelopes. Punch holes in all the decorated envelopes and sew to the binding tape. Create a closure for the book with a snap and twill ribbon.

the process

Vintage Envelope Card

BY CAROL

Tear a slit in a vintage envelope. Insert a tag and a framed vintage image. Attach the envelope to the front of a card.

the
process

The Family She Left Behind

BY LISA

Paint watercolor paper with diluted walnut ink. Let dry. *Use* for the title mat and border strip. To create the title tiles, rubber stamp a postal stamp on cardstock with sepia ink. Create a mask, then stamp the middle with script text using sand-colored ink. Color in the edge with colored pencils. Stamp with letter stamps using sepia ink. Adhere to cardboard (for thickness) and cut out. Shade the edges with black ink. Cover with VersaMark ink and add three layers of embossing enamel. Adhere with pop-dots. For the framed embellishment, attach a brass frame to stamped cardstock and cut out. Adhere findings to the center and fill with Diamond Glaze. Let dry, then adhere to the layout.

Photo Postage Cards
BY JENNIFER

Insert a small photo image into a WordArt document. Right click on the image, then select "Format Image." Change "Layout" to "behind text." Next, create several words using WordArt. Line them up over the image, changing the font to a color that will show up on the image. Print onto photo paper and cut out with postage-edge scissors.

the **process**

Secrets
BY JENNIFER

the process

Create a 12" x 12" envelope by piecing papers together. Run it through a printer to add "top secret" and other messages. Age with brown ink. Create a layout that is an 11 1/2" square and put a title at the bottom. Tear a hole in the envelope so the title shows through.

To create the faux postage, block off a small area on white cardstock with four sticky notes. Using a sponge, dab color for the background, then rubber stamp images. Remove the sticky notes and cut out with postage-edge scissors.

Idea to note: Create little "folders" to hide the journaling. When opened, the journaling pops up. To make the pop-ups, cut two slits about 3/4" long at the center of a folded piece of cardstock. Push this piece in towards the center and adhere journaling to the top surface.

chapter SIX

PLAY on WORDS

Ever wonder what to do with games or puzzles that are missing some pieces? Here's a creative way to use what's left: instead of throwing them out, strategically place them on your artwork and put a new spin on your artistic style.

Brandon
BY RENEE

the process

Cut out portions of a bingo card and adhere to background cardstock. Cut out BINGO title and replace letters by turning over the cutout number portions and stamping correct letters on them.

Artist
BY LISA

the process

For the corner embellishment, assemble one corner of a puzzle. A puzzle for 5-8 year olds works well because the pieces aren't too small. Flip the puzzle corner over and use a chalk inkpad to cover the pieces with ink. Let dry and rubber stamp with text stamps until covered. Let dry. Break off two pieces, then coat all with Diamond Glaze. When dry, adhere to light green cardstock with adhesive dots. To create the clock accent, stamp a clock image with black pigment ink and heat emboss. Trim to fit inside a 7gypsies finding with a pop-dot.

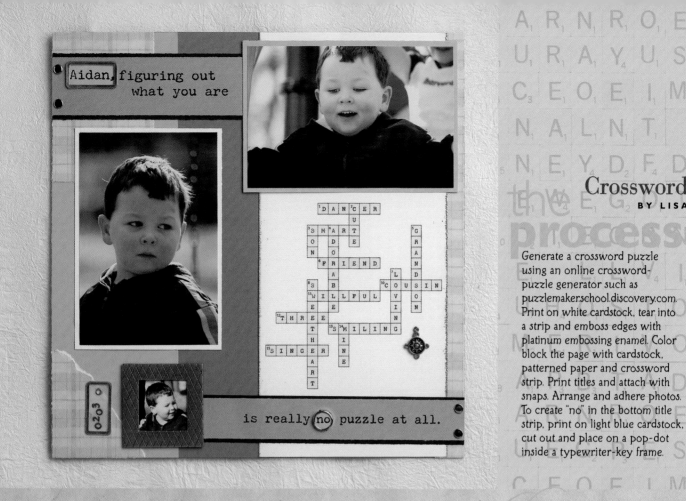

Aidan, figuring out what you are

is really (no) puzzle at all.

0203

Crossword
BY LISA

Generate a crossword puzzle using an online crossword-puzzle generator such as puzzlemaker.school.discovery.com. Print on white cardstock, tear into a strip and emboss edges with platinum embossing enamel. Color block the page with cardstock, patterned paper and crossword strip. Print titles and attach with snaps. Arrange and adhere photos. To create "no" in the bottom title strip, print on light blue cardstock, cut out and place on a pop-dot inside a typewriter-key frame.

Play
BY KRISTINA

Trim and adhere photos to layout. Stamp or write on vellum strips and affix to page. Add dominos to correspond with the number of items in the photos. Journal on vellum, using alphabet stamps for some of the words. Adhere to right-hand page. Stamp large letters onto vellum and adhere below the main picture. Add domino and alphabet charm accent.

2 shoes 4 stripes each = 8 stripes

4 stripes 1 pants

one costume

2 boots

12 stripes on 2 shoes and 1 pants to make you go faster. (like a tiger!)
super cool costume
2 shiny red boots
misc. hats, tools, bracelets and toys
countless walls to bounce off of
gallons of ENERGY
Imagination
all make up one

who loves to pretend

Play

Your Wish is My Command
BY RENEE

Seeds Shaker Box Accordion Book
BY CAROL

the **process**

Cut cardstock into two rectangles to form the covers. Cover the top piece with various papers. Create "coupons" by altering play money. Barely swipe the play money with acrylic paint. When dry, decorate with rubber stamps and write what the coupon is for. Safety pin the book together and score the front cover so it's easier to open.

the process

Determine which word(s) you would like to use to create a frame. Lay out, then measure both the outside and inside. Using those measurements, cut out a frame from foam board. Paint the inside and outside edges of the board. Paint and stamp background design on chipboard. Glue foam frame to background piece. Add elements to the inside of the frame, such as the seeds and dried flower used in this example. Cover with a transparency. Glue Scrabble letters around the perimeter. Place weights on the piece and allow to dry. Glue to the cover of a small accordion book.

Play Hard
BY RENEE

the **process**

Print a background of titles on cardstock. Stamp title onto blank ticket stubs and connect with brads. Add squares cut from various patterned papers underneath the photo mats for added interest.

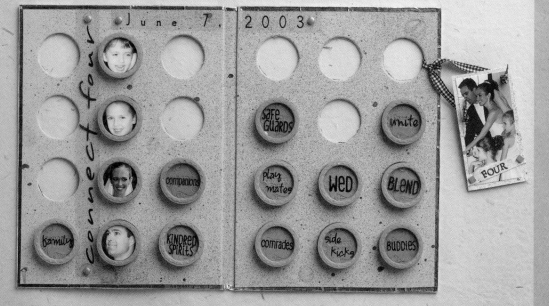

Connect Four
BY JENNIFER

the process

Paint two layers of ivory acrylic paint on a half-dollar coin holder. Paint Connect Four game pieces with blue and green paint. Using Diamond Glaze, adhere game pieces over several of the coin openings, and cut open the remaining openings. Print various words on a transparency and punch into small circles. Adhere words to the centers of the game pieces with Diamond Glaze. Attach title transparency pieces with rivets. Add photo to the side with ribbon.

Travel Journal
BY CAROL

the process

Scan a Scrabble board, convert to black and white and print onto text-weight paper. Print two copies and glue them to the front and back covers of a 5" x 7" accordion-fold book. Ink the covers with earth-toned and blue inks. Copy a vintage map onto a transparency. Cut out and adhere to the front cover. Add Scrabble letters to create a title and add travel-related accessories and a book clasp.

softly spoken

Sometimes it's best to let a photograph speak for itself. Not always does a title have to be the prominent feature on a work of art. Instead, let your title take a backseat and bring your photo to the forefront. Keep in mind a sage Spanish proverb: Don't speak unless you can improve on the silence. In other words, don't add a bold word when a soft, subtle one will do.

Winter Angel
BY TRACY

the**process**

Dry emboss a title using a stylus and template. Brush glue over title, being sure to cover all letters. Allow glue to dry until tacky, then adhere silver leafing using cotton gloves. Remove any excess with a soft brush. Print the word "winter" directly on the photo, then add to layout.

New **BY LISA**

Print title on cardstock, then add strips of patterned and pink paper. Adhere photo at an angle. Attach clasps to mat and adhere over photo. String twine through the clasps. Print baby's name on cardstock, put in a vellum envelope and adhere to a torn piece of patterned paper. Add the ring to symbolize a baby's ring. Adhere a small photo inside a silver frame, then fill with Diamond Glaze for a "keepsake" look.

Laugh
BY KRISTINA

Trim patterned papers and adhere to left side of layout. Stamp large letters on background. Add alphabet page pebbles over the photo. Stamp words on a small strip of vellum. Journal and stamp on another piece of vellum with very light ink and attach with brads.

Thoughts...Fantasies
BY CAROL

Lay lettering template backwards on a cutting mat or craft foam sheet. Lay vellum on top of template. Outline letters with a stylus and gently press centers of letters with stylus to "pop" them out. Remember you will be working from the back side of the vellum so the letters will be embossed in the reverse and will be done from right to left. Attach the titles with eyelets and sew them to other background papers with fiber.

Ironically, Leonardo DaVinci once commented, "Simplicity is the ultimate sophistication." One well-chosen word prominently displayed on a paper-art project can be the epitome of simplicity or utter classiness. Decide what one word best describes your subject and use that to make a powerful impact and make your handiwork simply sophisticated.

Quirky
BY RENEE
the process
Trim top portion of patterned paper and place on pop-dots. Adhere to striped patterned paper. Using pop-dots, adhere letter stickers to fiber pieces and secure under the top portion of patterned paper.

MAY 2003

Fate: An Anniversary Card
BY LISA

Rubber stamp images on ivory, gray and blue cardstocks using brown, green and gray inks. Trim into 1" x 1 1/2" rectangles. Print the word "FATE" on ivory cardstock and trim each letter into 1" x 1 1/2" rectangles. Age rectangles by stippling with ink and rubbing coordinating inks along the edges. Arrange rectangles on front of card. Tie charms to fibers, then run fibers through an eyelet and knot on the back. *the process*

Made your parents, after traveling the world, settle in the same town as mine.

Told your mother to hold you back in Kindergarten - so we ended up in the same graduating class.

Made sure all our early relationships (and one engagement) failed.

Made Daphne beg and plead with me to go out on that sticky, crowded Travers' night, when I really just wanted to go home.

Made you and your friends decide to go out on that sticky, crowded Travers' night.

Cleared away the 1,000 or so people crowding the patio at Gaffney's, so we could spot each other and start talking.

On this, our 10th Wedding Anniversary, I thank fate, and you, for the past 12 years...and all the years yet to come.

i love you.

Frolic
BY LISA

the process

Pour a 1" puddle of acrylic gesso on a palette. Pour a 1" puddle of platinum Lumiere paint next to it. Dip a large, soft brush so half of the brush has the gesso and half has Lumiere. Paint in a long swooping motion across the watercolor paper. Let dry, then trim. Stamp the word "frolic" with silver pigment ink. Heat emboss with silver embossing powder. Using direct-to-paper technique, cover a strip of watercolor paper with light green-ink. Stamp flower image in silver pigment ink and heat emboss. Cover with VersaMark ink and add one to three coats of embossing enamel. Bend to add cracks. Adhere to page with snaps. Attach a photo to a strip of watercolor paper and shade the edges with silver pigment ink.

FROLIC

Sculpture
BY KRISTINA

Print art image onto acid-free paper. Trim, mount on black cardstock and adhere to page. Trim patterned paper to make a border on the left side. Affix enlarged photo to the layout. Tear paper for corner embellishment and adhere a metal photo corner on the opposite corner. Stamp word on vellum and hand write its definition. Rubber stamp the date on the photo.

sculpture

Noun: a three-dimensional work of art.

dec '02

the process

Hilarious Frame

BY RENEE

the Process

Trim patterned papers to fit a white mat from a frame. Attach papers to the mat, then add strips of ribbon. Rubber stamp title and heat emboss. Punch stamped letters and attach to mat.

Electric Blue

BY JENNIFER

Adhere foil to the backs of several coin holders. Add electrical components as embellishments. Cut out the title letters and adhere with pop-dots.

Dauntless
BY JENNIFER

the process

Using a sharp knife, carefully scratch the title onto a photo. Create a tag that opens up to reveal the journaling.

Randomly swipe various dye inks directly onto a piece of glossy paper, start with the lightest color first. Between each color application, spray with alcohol and let dry, providing a marbled look. Hand write the word "Vivid" on scrap paper and temporarily attach over the glossy paper. Following the letters, punch several holes close together with an anywhere punch.

Vivid
BY JENNIFER

Reflection
BY CAROL

the process

Cut a mirror into small squares with a glass cutter or purchase pre-cut pieces. Apply letter stickers to the squares. Adhere the embellished mirrors to the layout with E-6000.

In the early 1900s, when people would try to sell horses, inaccurate information was often given about the condition of a horse's mouth. To get the truth, the buyer wouldn't rely on the seller's testimony. Instead, he would go "straight to the horse's mouth" and find out for himself. For most people, when they want to tell things like they really are, they'll use their own words and not rely on others to speak for them. So as you create works of art, employ your own handwriting and journaling to add a personal touch and to ensure that the truth is told!

Walk with Angels
BY JENNIFER

the process

Write "walk in love" and "walk with angels" with a glue pen. Quickly press leafing onto glue and use a brush to remove any excess. Journal on torn vellum and attach at the bottom of a photo. Add stitching to the right side of the layout. **Idea to note:** Use gold and copper leafing pens to change the color of the metal frame.

Supergirl
BY KRISTINA

the process

Create a background from various patterned papers. Use ribbon for a photo corner accent. Frame an alphabet charm with a metal-rimmed tag and adhere to layout. Write and stamp journaling on vellum, then add to page, hiding the adhesive under the alphabet charms. **Idea to note:** Add flair to journaling by mixing handwriting, stickers, stamps and embellishment letters.

2003: Year in Review

BY KRISTINA

the process

Cover the envelope with patterned papers. Ink
the edges and age as desired. Adhere ribbon and
heart embellishment to the flap. Cover with words.
To create the tag, adhere patterned paper and photo to chipboard.
Cover the rest of the chipboard with titles and journaling.
Tie ribbon and fibers through a hole in the top.

handwriting

I will never forget my grandmother's signature—the one I
always see at the bottom of all her cards and notes. And I won't
forget the hand in which my mother jotted down notes for me
and left on the kitchen table, telling me where she had gone. It
is their own unique signature, similar to a fingerprint. No one
else on this planet has that same one.

My wish is for my children to never forget my unique
handwriting and to know that every time I made a scrapbook
page for them, where I included a little memory, thought or
other bit of information, it was done in my own handwriting,
especially for them. No one can duplicate it. No one can use it.
There is no font like my own handwriting, and there never will
be. My hand is for me and my kids alone. And when they see

my handwriting, they know it was me who wrote it and me
who wanted to make sure it was written down.

Your handwriting changes with your mood. When you are in a
hurry, it becomes sloppier and less articulate. When you are
being wise or expressing deep emotion, it becomes more
script-like. It becomes large, bubbly, bold and thick when you
are happy and having fun. It is so important in the day of
technology to preserve one of the unique ways in which we
have to express ourselves and leave a part of ourselves behind.

Kristina

age old WORDS

Aging is a popular technique used to add a touch of yesteryear and nostalgia to an otherwise new project. Since not everyone owns old, antique embellishments or memorabilia, learn from these artists how to create a rich patina that will enhance your titles and journaling.

Through the Eyes of a Child
BY CAROL

the process

Follow manufacturer's directions to transfer photos and computer-generated journaling onto fabric. Stamp or stencil titles, letters or words with permanent fabric ink. Heat-set for permanency, being careful not to melt the Lazertran images. Age fabric and images with vintage-colored fabric inks.

Pillow-sew the fronts and backs of each page together, leaving the spine edge open. Turn right side out and bind the spine edge with twill. When all pages are complete, machine stitch buttonholes in each page and tie together with twill.

Print a photo onto the uncoated side of ink jet canvas paper. Wrap the image around chipboard and secure with mini brads. Sponge walnut ink around the edges to age. Spray fabric, ribbon, lace and paper with walnut ink to age.

Using the fine-point nib of a wood-burning tool, write words on a strip of wood. Burn the edges to age and attach to the layout with eyelets.

Three Sisters
BY TRACY

Print title onto a patch of calico. Iron to set the ink. Print the journaling onto cardstock, then age with a weak mix of walnut ink. With a stronger mix of walnut ink, paint the embossed paper and allow to dry. Paint the stitched tin tile and charm with gold acrylic paint. Sand the edges of the tile, then stamp the date. Sew the title and journaling blocks to the background.

the process

chapter eleven
spoken clearly

Ever go through a drive-thru and the voice on the other end of the speaker is a garbled mess of syllables? Not only is it frustrating, but it also causes both parties to shout. Simply put, having things clear and easily understandable makes all situations more pleasant. Check out how these artists use fresh, clearly-stated words to enhance their projects by using transparencies, mica chips and small laminate pieces.

Pout
BY RENEE

the process

Trim patterned paper to size, then antique and sand the edges. Stamp title onto mica chips and attach together with eyelets. Attach to page with twine. Glaze the back of a few mica chips, then attach flower patterned paper for a feminine accent.

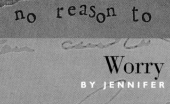

faith, family, and friends.

no reason to

Worry
BY JENNIFER

For the title piece, stamp the word "worry" with permanent ink on clear laminate. After it is dry, remove laminate backing and shake on leafing. Press leafing to the laminate with your fingers and remove any excess with a brush. Mat on printed paper and adhere to page. Using a black permanent pen, hand write messages on the laminate, then add leafing following the same steps as above. Make the mini photo frame in the same manner. Add a bit of adhesive to the envelope closure, then add leafing to tie the page together.

the process

From: ken...

I will always be there to make you laugh even when you are on the verge of tears.

You are the best at what you do, and even if you won't admit it, I will.

We will travel enough to escape reality frequently because we both love to.

You will always have someone to lean on in difficult times.

Faith, family, and friends.

no reason to

WORRY

remarkable YOu

eveR

For "Remarkable You," stamp images onto glossy paper and heat-set until dry. Brayer ink over the top to create a resist image. Print journaling for card onto a transparency and fold in half. Attach the glossy paper to the transparency with adhesive dots.

Create the background for the "Thank You" card by stamping an image onto glossy paper with a watermark inkpad. Dry with a heat-embossing gun. Brayer ink onto the surface. Sew 'thank you' portion onto bottom of image. Mount entire piece to the inside of a folded transparency. Set eyelets and use ribbon for a closure.

Print title for "Best Ever" onto a transparency. Stamp images and heat emboss. Fold transparency in half with a bone folder. Attach folded white cardstock in center and punch holes through both the cardstock and the transparency. Tie together with ribbon.

Cards
BY RENEE

the process

There are many things that make up the traditional family. The first being husband and wife. When Thomas and I married, we were instantly "family"...bound together by God, law, and love. We were truly content to be a family this way. We lived for almost 4 years before realizing, we needed something else. We needed the addition of a child to be complete (so we thought) our "family". We became pregnant with our firstborn, Brandon. We instantly bonded with our miracle and felt that our family was complete. And so it was...for 3 additional years. Along came Zachary, a companion for Brandon...someone with whom he could play with and spend countless hours being brothers together. I couldn't wait to bring him home, to experience our "family" of four. I knew that THIS was what family was...this had to be it. Then 2 years later, we became pregnant again, hoping all along that it was to be the girl we both desired. And, to our surprise, it was. We now had a girl to complete our family. We had someone that the boys could grow with, share with, love, and protect. Thomas and I both felt that this was the completion of our family. And so it was...

But with this completion also came the realization that family does not consist entirely of family members, but rather moments of time...memories...experiences...shared together. With the union of our souls came a moment of time that we will never forget. That made us family. With the growth of our marriage from year to year came experiences...that made us family. With the birth of our first son came renewed love. That made us family. With the additional birth of each child, came joy and completion. Those additions made us family. With each loss, with each gain, with each celebration, with each birth, with each tear, with each laugh, with each smile, with each hug, with each embrace, we have become family. We have become a unit...a measure...a joint celebration of people put on earth to experience life together. And as time goes on, we will grow together...hopefully closer becoming more and more what a family truly should be.

Family
BY RENEE

Crop photo to fit on background cardstock. Place strips of patterned paper along top portion of the cardstock. Add letter stickers and rub-ons for additional words. Attach vellum over entire piece with rivets. Print journaling and title on transparency and bind it to the bottom portion of the layout with hinging tape.

the process

You Belong to Me
BY KRISTINA

Create a string and button envelope from a transparency. Cut one sheet of vellum and one sheet of transparency to fit inside the envelope. Journal on the vellum and stamp a title on the transparency. Slip the layers into the envelope, putting memorabilia between the two layers.

the process

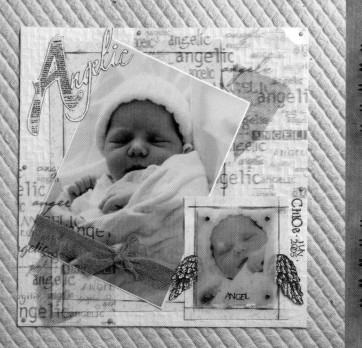

Stick a printed definition to a sheet of clear laminate. Soak in water for one minute, then partially rub the paper off. Cut out the letter "A" and mat on white cardstock. For the bottom photo, print the photo on enhanced matte paper. Do the same with the laminate as you did for the "A." Adhere to paper with brads. For the transparency background pieces, create a document with the word "angelic" repeated many times in various fonts and font sizes. Tear some edges and add to layout with brads.

Angelic
BY JENNIFER

Prayer Journal
BY RENEE

Collage pieces of paper and definitions on cardstock bases. Attach microscope slides over the top with paper glaze and eyelets. Connect all the slides together using wire. *Use pop-dots to attach the slides to the front of the journal.* **Idea to note:** *Use journal ribbon as a place holder.*

the process

the
process

Timeless
BY KRISTINA

Collage various patterned papers to create the background for the journaling. Rubber stamp clocks on the papers. Adhere a strip of vellum down the middle of the page. Cut a transparency in half. Stamp a large word with chalk ink on the left side of the transparency. Cut 2" from the second half of the transparency and journal with permanent ink. Stamp "timeless" on a small piece of vellum. Adhere the transparencies and title under a strip of cardstock. Stamp "timeless" with large alphabet stamps on the left side of the layout, then cover with vellum.

Tender
BY JENNIFER

Cut a 1/8" thick clear plastic piece to 12" x 12". Paint on a small amount of white acrylic paint and wipe away quickly, leaving a slightly messy look. Cut out the title ("tender") from cardstock. Temporarily adhere to the plastic and spray several layers of frosted - glass finish over the top. When dry, remove the letters and trace the edges with a white pen. Print journaling onto a transparency and scribble on the back - behind keywords - to highlight. To create the faux wax seals, ink a shadow alphabet stamp with VersaMark, then press into a dab of hot glue. Remove stamp when cool. Paint with gold and copper leafing pens.

the process

Extraordinary, tender loving care.

I can't better describe the emotions between Mike and Audrey. They are the best of buddies, the closest of pals.

When I married Ken and became Audrey's step mom, I knew Audrey and I would feel connected and close. I knew Mike would grow to adore her. But I never imagined how much.

Mike and Audrey's relationship is extraordinary. Simply amazing. They giggle. They laugh. They bring out the best in each other...pulling one and other out of their shy, quiet shells. I have never seen a little girl adore their uncle as much as Audrey does Mike. And I have never seen Mike smile as big as he does when he is with Audrey.

Extraordinary.

extraordinary
tender
loving care...

JUL 03

TLC

Art Journal
BY CAROL
the process

Paint and rubber stamp the covers of a pre-purchased wooden book. Cover with collage paper and add elements, including pre-painted wooden letters. Allow to dry overnight. Melt clear encaustic wax in a clean tin can (tuna-can size) on a warm griddle. Paint melted wax over the book cover. Smooth with a warm, travel-size iron (non-steam works best).

TIPS FOR ENCAUSTIC WAX PAINTING:

1. Encaustic wax is generally a combination of beeswax and resin. To purchase wax, check with your local craft store or online sources.

2. Special tools such as an iron and a heated stylus with interchangeable tips are manufactured by Arts Encaustic International. You may be able to purchase these tools from the same source as the wax.

3. Working with hot wax is messy. Wear old clothing and cover your work surface with paper.

4. Keep a fire extinguisher handy, just in case. Wax should not be too hot; it melts at about 140 degrees.

5. A wax finish over a collage piece is exceptionally beautiful, producing a translucent, old-world look.

Mica Cards
BY RENEE

TIME FLIES

Rubber stamp various words onto cardstock scraps and heat emboss. Create resist pieces by embossing with clear powder and swiping walnut ink over the top. Punch squares out of various stickers and embossed papers. Attach to page, applying accents on top of several squares.

THANK YOU

Find words in a magazine to express your sentiment. Tear or cut them out and mount between two mica sheets. Secure with an eyelet. Cover the front of a cardstock card with patterned paper. Antique the edges with ink. Tie fiber to the card and hang the words from the fiber.

I'M SO PROUD OF YOU

Create a resist image by stamping alphabet letters onto glossy paper using VersaMark or another resist inkpad. Allow to dry completely. Using a brayer, apply dye ink over the dried surface until blended. Set eyelets in the corners of mica chips and tie together. Place over a photo that has been sanded.

the process

Clear Bookmarks
BY RENEE

Print quotations onto a transparency and trim to bookmark size. Swipe the back of each bookmark with liquid glue, allowing to dry until clear and tacky. Rub silver leafing onto the tacky portion and brush off any excess with a stiff-bristled brush. Punch a hole at the top and use ribbon for a tie.

the process

twelve
printing
words from the
press

Who would've imagined the invention of the printing press in 1450 would impact our scrapbook pages and paper art projects? More than ever, artists are using printing press techniques—albeit using a computer—on their masterpieces. For this chapter, the artists have ingeniously devised creative ways to use computer-generated words on their pieces. So start using the knowledge Johann Gutenberg passed on to us to print your very own cutting-edge creations.

Keaton
BY CAROL

If you have photos which include writing or printing, use a comparable computer font to complement your project. In this sample, the font resembles the stencil lettering in the photo. Format the lettering to create top and bottom borders and print them onto cardstock. To create the title letters, computer generate stencil-type letters on red cardstock. Scan and print them on a transparency. Cut out the letters and mount on the layout. **Idea to note:** To give the photos a translucent look, scan and print onto transparencies.

Memory Journal
BY LISA

Print background words on white cardstock in light-gray ink. Adhere to the front of a composition book. Collage additional ephemera to the cover. Age the edges with a sepia-black inkpad. Print the words "Memory Journal" onto red cardstock, adhere under a nickel square and fill with Diamond Glaze. For the "photos" frame, rubber stamp a frame image in VersaMark and heat emboss with silver embossing powder.

the process

We'd made plans to meet Terry and the kids at Hembree Park. Aidan and I got there early, and he ran right over to his favorite thing – the tire swing. All by himself, my poor little guy looked so lonely and sad.

Then Terry and Kim showed up with the kids. They all took turns squeezing into the swing - we have no clue how they all fit. Add in a little push from Mom, and you couldn't have erased that happy smile off Aidan's face if you tried!

April 2003

Tire swingin' is so much better with **FRIENDS**

FRIENDS

Friends
BY LISA

the process

Print title and subtitle strips, printing the title in black and subtitles in gray. Tear, then shade the edges with black pigment ink. Attach with glue or brads. Print the journaling block, shade edges and attach with brads. Attach a strip of red cardstock with staples for added interest. To make the title letters and date block, create a text box, changing the background color to black and the text to white. Type the text, ensuring the black area around it is large enough for the final mounting. Print onto glossy photo paper. Cut out and adhere to tags. Mount tags on pop-dots.

Strum
BY TRACY

Create the title by layering text boxes. Print title and journaling onto cardstock and cut around the letters with an X-Acto knife, allowing a photo to be slipped underneath. Print the title and journaling back to back on a second sheet in the exact same position. Trim to size and layer over the top. Attach the two pieces with eyelets, then score the edge of the top layer to allow it to fold back.

process

Notes from Grandma
BY JENNIFER

the process

Cut a front and back cover from plastic canvas. Cut two shorter pieces of the canvas to make the inside pockets. Age the canvas by sponging with brown ink. Stamp with Krylon Clear Coat to protect. Stitch together the stationery pockets with embroidery floss. Add ribbon and buttons for the binding and closure. Stamp words onto buttons with permanent ink. Print words on a photo to use on the cover. To create the stationery, lighten a photo in Photoshop®. Add words in light colors. Frame and title. Print, fold in half and store in the stationery pocket. Print similar words on the envelopes so they match.

Determination
BY RENEE

Cut wire mesh to 8 1/2" x 11".
Clip off any stray edges with
wire clippers. Create a photo
mat by rotating text boxes in
an editing program to create a
frame. Add definitions and
rub-ons. Tie or sew elements
to the wire mesh background.

the process

Peace and Sleep
BY JENNIFER

Run photos through a printer to print words directly on photos. For the tin embellishment that houses baby booties, paint a CD-tin white. Print words onto tissue paper and let dry. Rub a thin layer of *Perfect Paper Adhesive* on the lid, then add tissue. Smooth out the tissue with an additional layer of adhesive. Once dry, dab with brown dye ink and red pigment ink. Let dry. Adhere bottom of tin to a piece of plastic canvas that has been dabbed with red pigment ink and embossed in red. Use brads to hold the canvas to the page and use ribbon to hold the tin in place.

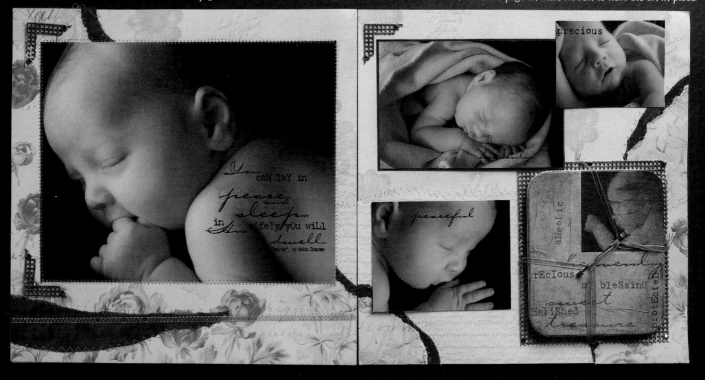

Dreams
BY TRACY

In a photo-editing program, create an edge on the photos and add a cracked finish. Import the image into Microsoft™ Word, add the title with a text box, change the line to "no line" and the fill to "no fill," then layer it over the photo. Print on an ink jet transparency. Create the background using WordArt. Type in desired text and rotate into position. Select Fill/Fill Effects and fill with colors. Duplicate the words and arrange on the page. Attach the transparencies over the background. Emboss thin strips of cardstock with a label maker and add to the bottom.

100% Authentic
BY CAROL

Attach a piece of lightweight, light-colored fabric to an 8 1/2" x 11" piece of cardstock using double-sided tape. Make sure the fabric is pulled taut, without wrinkles or bulges and make sure the cardstock is flat. Print as usual. Remove the fabric from the cardstock and create your layout. To print on twill tape, type words on one line, no larger than the height of the tape. Print on standard copy paper. Position the twill tape over the printed words and secure with double-sided tape. Print on the paper again, but this time the text will print on the tape.

CAROL'S TIPS

- 100% cotton fabric works best; polyester tends to bleed a little when printed with an ink jet printer.

- Buying precut quilting pieces (fat quarters) is a great way to have variety without a large monetary investment.

- Fabric may also be ironed onto freezer paper to create a "carrier," or it can be purchased at some fabric stores already attached to a removable backing.

- Printers are sensitive creatures; test this method prior to doing the final project!

CONTENTS:
40% TOMBOY
30% GIRLIE
20% MISCHIEVOUS
10% UNIQUE &
    UNPREDICTABLE

SIZE: 3T

CARE INSTRUCTIONS:
HUG OFTEN
LOVE UNCONDITIONALLY
ENCOURAGE INDIVIDUALITY
ENJOY FOR A LIFETIME

100% AUTHENTIC

Creating Layered Text in Microsoft® Word

BY JENNIFER AND TRACY

One of our favorite things to do is download and play with fonts on the computer. A word-processing program like Word offers all sorts of tools to create interesting titles and manipulate fonts. To begin, create a text box, which allows you to have complete control over the size of the piece you create.

Then follow these steps to create layered text using text boxes:

1. Set the page size for the paper you are printing on. A 12" x 12" printer will print directly onto the background paper. A smaller printer will print 8 1/2" x 12" (most printers will print longer than standard sizes).

2. Select Insert/Text Box from the menu and draw a text box (this can be changed later). Enter and format the text.

3. Right click on the edge of the text box and select "Format Text Box." In here, you can change the fill color, outside line, size, etc. Can also drag the corners of the box to resize. Select no fill and no line to create a layered title.

4. Repeat the above steps until all the text is on the page.

5. Stagger and layer the boxes until you have the look you want. To change the order of layered text, right click the edge of the text box and select "Order."

HINT: To create "white" text, select the desired fill color and change the text color to white. Print on white paper and the printer will print a colored text box and give the appearance of a white printed title (see "School Book" in chapter 1).

Creating Layered Text in Microsoft® WordArt

WordArt provides more fill options and has more flexibility in altering text.

1. Select the WordArt and Drawing toolbar in View/Toolbars.

2. Select the WordArt tool, then enter text and select a font. Change the word style after the text has been entered by using the options on the WordArt toolbar.

3. Now the text will be treated as a graphic. You can alter the size by dragging on the corners. Rotate, change the text to a vertical format, center or experiment with the other options using the WordArt toolbar.

4. To change the color, select "Fill Color" from the drawing toolbar. Here you can select solid colors or "fill effects" for the gradient effect as seen in the "Dreams" layout. Select your own colors or one of the preset combinations. Select no line if you do not want a border around the text.

5. Once the WordArt boxes are created, move them around following the same instructions for text boxes.

6. WordArt also allows you to reverse the lettering so you can cut it out or transfer it onto a different medium. To reverse text, select Draw/Flip Horizontal.

These are just a few of the options to create interesting titles in software by manipulating text. Explore different looks by using different types of fonts.

Bag It!

BY DEBBIE

the process

Cut freezer paper and fabric to 8 1/2" x 11". Iron the shiny side of the freezer paper to the fabric. Run fabric through the printer so the words print on the fabric. Turn under and hem the top edge of the bag (this will be the 11" side). With right sides together, stitch the 8 1/2" sides together to form a tube. Stitch the bottom edge closed. Stitch triangles in the bottom sides to form gussets. Crease the corners of the sack. Cut a piece of chipboard to fit in the bottom for stability. For a roll down closure, apply eyelets on both sides of the bag. Tie closed with ribbon.

DEBBIE'S IDEAS:

- Cover the "Grad Bag" with quotations about the future and the graduate's high school and year. Fill with money, coupons to favorite places and other goodies.

- Cover an entire page with random letters and numbers, then go back and insert "hidden messages" into the text. Make them both upper and lower case so they are more difficult to find.

- Cover the entire page with words or phrases that include the word "key." This bag is perfect for a Valentine or anniversary gift.

words to Impress

Whoever said you only have one chance to make a first impression certainly didn't know anything about paper arts or rubber stamping. In this chapter, the artists offer several ideas for making a second, third or even fourth impression on your masterpieces. Explore these artistic ways to emboss and add texture to your projects.

Nature Folio
BY CAROL

the process

Stamp letters and images on copper using petroleum jelly as the "ink." Immerse copper into a diluted solution of liver of sulfur. Rinse in clean water and dry. Cut chipboard into small tiles and wrap stamped metal images around the chipboard. Glue "tiles" to the cover of a handmade, hardbound folio, leaving small spaces between the tiles. Allow to dry. Carefully fill the spaces with Diamond Glaze. Dry thoroughly, then paint over the glaze with a silver leaf pen to resemble grout lines. Using a stylus, deboss the letters to create texture and dimension.

The day the Lord created *hope* was probably the same day he created *spring.* —Bern Williams

Hope
BY RENEE

Create a background from squares cut from patterned paper. *Use a melting pot to create "puddles" of Ultra Thick Embossing Enamel that can be impressed upon with rubber stamps. When using a melting pot, try adding regular embossing powder to clear embossing enamel to create a specialized color and mixture.*

the process

field notes

research dragonflies

Reverse print the title on a sheet of cardstock. Cut out the title and adhere the cutout letters at the top of the layout. Tear several openings in the background cardstock, then attach metal shim to the back. Stamp words on shim with metal stamps. Place foil behind the cutout title.

Exhilaration
BY TRACY

Tear faux leather into squares with irregular edges. Heat each piece with an embossing gun, then press an un-inked letter stamp into the leather. Allow to cool. Gently rub the surface of the letter with metallic rub-ons. Use the same technique for the flower accents. Crumple an empty seed packet and rub with brown ink. Embellish the packet and hide journaling inside. Using a stippling brush and brown ink, age all background papers and ticket stubs.

the
process

Backyard Paradise
BY JENNIFER

chapter fourteen repeat after me

Do you remember your school teachers telling you the more you repeat and review something, the easier it will be to recall later? Think of how quickly you learned the words to your favorite songs or how quickly you memorized your first love's phone number because you called it several times a day. There is power in repetition. And when words are repeated on a card, scrapbook page or journal there can be no doubt about the message. Take note how these artists repeat words to make a lasting impression.

Time
BY TRACY

Sand the stitched tin tiles, then coat with gesso and acrylic paint. Sand the edges of the tiles, ink the edges and stamp images with permanent ink. Attach to the layout with metal glue or adhesive dots. Print journaling onto an ink jet transparency and tear (start the tear with scissors). Tear the patterned paper and layer over the background.

the process

Time moves at a startling speed - days, months years pass seemingly in an instant. As time passes we gather memories to remember the times we have laughed, cried, rejoiced, feared and worried. I have watched time take you from my arms as a baby and bring you to me now as this beautiful, composed little girl full of life, laughter, joy, fears and worry. The transition from being six to turning seven concerned you. Perhaps you also feel that time is passing too fast, that tomorrow you may wake up and find yourself as a grown up. *Time moves at a startling speed* - days, months years pass seemingly in an instant. I wish I could capture time in a bottle for you and hold you at a point of time where you feel nothing but joy. Time does not allow that and so I savour each passing day spent with you, teaching you, loving you. Take each day and hold on to it in your memory because there you can make time seemingly stand still as I can do when I hold you and close my eyes and remember so many precious moments. *Time moves at a startling speed* – treasure each passing moment and value each passing day, month and year. Your last day being six – 31st July 2003.

Embrace
BY JANELLE

the process

Cover an old book with paper. Embellish the cover with words and objects that reflect the book's theme. To create the "Hold" page, use an iron-on transfer to transfer photos onto material. Sew material to the page to form a pocket. For the "Ball" page, print thoughts about the picture onto a transparency, then bind the transparency into the book. To create a frame for the photo, tear out the centers from several pages at varying widths and age the edges with ink. For the "Time" page, adhere tags to the page with PVA. Write on them in a "swirly" pattern. Stamp the word "time" on the twill tape and adhere it to the page using clock faces, age the opposite page by rubbing a chalk inkpad over the top. Adhere watch parts with PVA. Cut a hole in the book through about 50 pages so a mini bottle will fit inside.

Dream
BY KRISTINA

Stamp large letters on cardstock. Adhere trimmed and torn patterned papers. Attach stamped image with brads. Add metal alphabet charms, letter stickers and fiber. Write on an enlarged photo with permanent marker.

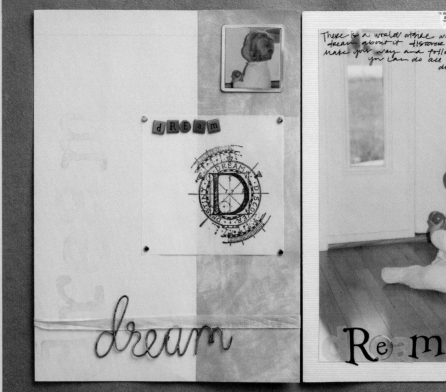

Love
BY JANELLE

Cut cardstock into small strips. Stamp "love" at the bottom of each one. Overlap the strips to create a heart shape and adhere in place.

the
process

56

Art Journal
BY TRACY

the process

Rubber stamp a perforated postage-stamp sheet to create the background using the template provided with the perforated paper. Add words and floral images. Scan the stamped sheet and load into a word or graphics program, such as Microsoft® Publisher. Create text boxes and add text ("Art" and "Art is pictures straight from the heart"). Print in reverse onto transfer paper. Iron onto cardstock following the manufacturer's instructions. The transfer sheet may not peel off as easily as it might on fabric, but this all adds to the look. Remove the cover from a spiral notebook by gently pulling the spirals open. Use it as a template to mark the holes on the cardstock piece. Cut the cardstock to size, then thread the new cover onto the spirals. Sand the edges and coat the entire cover with Perfect Paper.

the process

Serenity
BY JENNIFER

Cut cardboard into two 10" x 12" pieces. Add paper. Punch holes for the elastic pieces. Repeat the word "serenity" around the piece using various letters. Attach the pieces of cardboard together with ribbon.

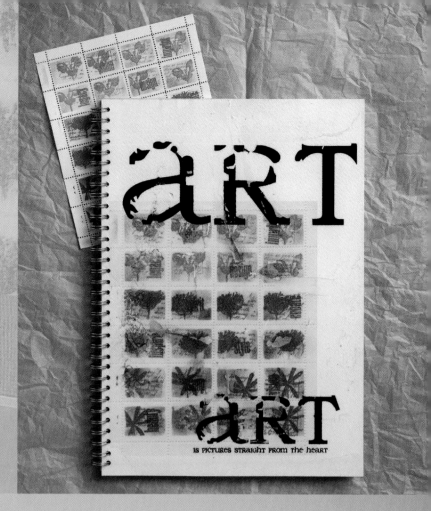

Dear Artists,

I'm sent through harsh territories and stuffed into small spaces just so you can read and enjoy me. I contain some of the most heartfelt sentiments and expressions. But once you read me, don't just hide me away or worse yet, throw me away. Instead, recycle me or preserve the cherished words by using me as part of or inspiration for your works of art.

Sincerely,
Your Letters

Dearest Karen BY JENNIFER *the process*

Cut patterned papers at angles and sew paper strips to the top edges. Line up all the pieces and clip with paper clips to temporarily hold in place while sewing the edges together. Rubber stamp words onto the papers. Tuck letters into pockets. Add pressed flowers and put Poemstones on top.

Snips and Snails
BY KRISTINA

the process

Print text onto a transparency. Attach patterned papers to background, then attach transparency with brads. Adhere torn paper corners to the layout and add a photo to the top of the transparency. Loop beads and charms to a large clip, then sew it to the page. Layer an envelope, torn paper, a photo and ribbon to chipboard to create the right-hand page.

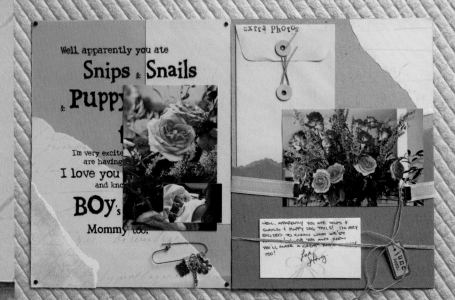

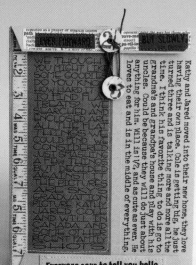

Inside Out
BY DEBBIE

the process

The entire letter to Kyle is printed on the outside of the envelope and the inside is packed with flat treats, such as gift certificates, photos, cash, calling cards, gift cards, candy, gum, etc. Construct a letter using several paragraphs that fit together in random directions. Print a few words on different colors of paper and stitch them on the envelope. Instead of trying to fit the letter on a specific template, use the entire sheet and cut off a strip from each corner. The center strip on each side forms the envelope flaps. Close the envelope with a string closure.

The "always" envelope—made with canvas paper—is an anniversary card and is covered with lyrics from the recipients' favorite song, "Always." Don't forget to add the address and return address.

Graduation Tin
BY CAROL

the process

Wrap the outside of a tin with handwriting paper and a stamped title. Add embellishments and a tag. Computer generate a note for the inside. Rubber stamp the note with related images. Machine stitch the note to handmade, leather-looking paper. Create folds to resemble a Roman shade, and punch tiny holes between the fold lines. Weave waxed linen through the holes and tie knots at both ends. Add a charm and insert into tin.

Used extensively in the 18th and 19th centuries, calling cards were a way for visitors to announce their arrival. Let these designers show how you, too, can include a calling card on your artwork to let your audience know you've been there. And on the calling card or just somewhere on the project, be sure to add your initials. Just as a cattleman brands his property, you can "brand" your original pieces in a much less painful way!

ZKB
BY RENEE

Create a photo mat that has each child's name directly under his or her photo. Stencil their initials on another portion of the layout using acrylic paint. Attach stencils to the bottom and swipe with ink that coordinates with the font color. Tuck journaling inside a glassine envelope.

the process

AW
BY KRISTINA

the process

Adhere various patterned papers to background paper. Wrap fibers around an enlarged photograph, adding a metal ring to the knot in front. Tuck a "calling card" behind the fibers. Sew on buttons and attach metal letters. Paint initials on vellum and adhere to the left side, hiding the glue behind the photographs. Print out words onto transparency and attach with brads. Attach the metal letters to the inside of an acrylic box.

JMA
BY JENNIFER

the Glue strips of patterned paper to a rectangle of paper and run through the printer. Machine stitch around the strips and rub with metallic rub-ons. Add eyelets, charm and wire.

Monogram Tag
BY CAROL
the process

Cover a painted wooden letter with fiber. Adhere to a painted metal-rimmed tag. Cut handmade paper into a rectangle and embellish with monogrammed tag, brads, string and a small, filled glass bottle.

It's All About Me
BY DEBBIE

Cut a tag from cardboard. Cut fabric to fit on the tag. Stitch fabric, paper and ribbon to the tag. Embroider a "D" onto fabric, then stitch it to the tag. To print on ribbon, arrange text to fit on ribbon and print a sample copy. Attach ribbon over the text using double-sided tape and run it through the printer again. Loop ribbon through the hole of the tag.

song lyrics

Gustav Mahler once stated, "If a composer could say what he had to say in words, he would not bother trying to say it in music." Sometimes words aren't enough to express a feeling or emotion. But one can usually find a song to express what he or she is feeling. Let music be the inspiration for your next creative opus. You're sure to strike a chord!

Remember When
BY CAROL

the process

Create a fabric envelope pouch to house an old record. Image transfer lyrics and photos onto transfer paper. Follow manufacturer's directions to adhere to fabric. Quilt pieces onto the front of the pouch. Add buttons and enamel plate aged with alcohol inks.

Remember when I first met you, my lips were so afraid to say "I love you"?

Remember when, to my surprise, the heaven in my heart leaped into your eyes?

Remember how much I cried tears of joy to think you were mine?

Darling, down deep inside, I still feel that feeling divine.

I loved you then and I still do: I can't remember when I didn't love you.

Love

Life Card
BY JENNIFER

the process

Cover postage-stamp paper with acrylic paint. Shrink a scan of sheet music and print on scrap paper. Temporarily adhere postage-stamp paper over the scrap paper and print again. Adhere to front of a card. Add handmade paper, song lyrics and definition. Punch holes along the top of the card and tie with fiber. Add the word bead through the fiber. Print lyrics on the front of a CD envelope. Wipe wet ink off the clear plastic.

life

...talk in everlasting words... ...dedicate them all to me... ...and I will give you all my life...

Lighthouse
BY TRACY

Scan sheet music and the main photo. Use a program such as Photoshop 7® to alter and layer the photo, sheet music and words to create the background. Print in black and white. Mount photo on black cardstock and position over the background.

my lighthouse

And you're the lighthouse leading me home
Guiding me through every storm
You're the sun that shines on my face
The warming embrace
The light of my days
You're the lighthouse

love

I Have Been Blessed
BY JANELLE

the process

Print the main title onto printed paper, then adhere it to the cover with PVA. Print photos onto a transparency and trim to fit inside protective slide covers. Rub letters onto brads, following manufacturer's instructions. Rub olive-colored pigment ink over the edges of the cover to give it a worn look. Age the text boxes with inks, as well, and age the pink daisy paper with walnut ink.

For the "laughing" page, attach the photo strips together with eyelets and waxed linen. Age the word strips by rubbing ink on the edges and adding color over the top with a brayer. Print the word "laughing" onto a transparency, then mount on a page that has been colored with pastel and watercolor pencils. Slip an embellished tag into the glassine envelope that is bound in the journal.

White Family Music Journal
BY KRISTINA

the process

Alter the cover of a 7gypsies "gated journal" with stamps, stickers, alphabet charms and other embellishments. Design the inside pages to reflect the song-lyric/CD theme. Include a title page and a few information pages if desired. Use various mediums to decorate the pages like paints, rubber stamps, papers, stickers, tags, charms, color copies of CDs, etc. Be sure to document why the CDs/song lyrics are important or meaningful.

WORD on the STREET

Travel down the street and you'll be bombarded by words: billboards, graffiti, marquees, traffic signs, homemade signs and store signs. Words are everywhere! Don't just be a casual observer; instead, use the "word on the street" as inspiration for cards, books and scrapbook pages.

Marquee Cards
BY DEBBIE

the process

Fold cardstock to form a card. Cut strips of cardstock to approximately 3/8" wide and to the same length as the card. Sew the strips to the card to hold letter "tiles." Make letter "tiles" from chipboard and stamp with letters. Slip letters into slots to hold the message in place.

Fresh and New
BY RENEE

the process

Create an advertisement for love. Crumple to age, then tear off a few tags from the bottom. Staple some to the layout.

Signs of Our Daily Life

BY TRACY

the
process

Hand cut the title with an X-Acto knife. Mount the photos using different sizes of squares and rectangles. Ink the title and the edges of the layout.

5 Days in Portland

BY JANELLE

the process

Fold a map to create an accordion-fold book with pockets. Tuck tags, trinkets and souvenirs into the pockets. Cover two pieces of cardboard with paper and adhere to the front and back flaps of the map to form the covers. Tie the book closed with ribbon.

nineteen
the GIFT of words

How often have you stewed about and worked yourself into a tizzy trying to think of what to give your mom for Mother's Day or your best friend for her birthday? Fret no more! Simply transform an otherwise generic item into a prized possession through the gift of words. Never underestimate the value of sincere expressions from a loved one as you embellish with heartfelt sentiments what will become the perfect present.

Light Tomorrow
BY JENNIFER

the process
Stamp words onto white tissue paper with pigment ink. Tear the word out and use a glue stick to lightly adhere it around a candle. Carefully apply heat with a heat gun to melt the tissue into the candle. (The tissue will disappear.) Don't apply too much heat or the wax will drip. Keep adding stamped words and images one at a time.

Live the Life
BY RENEE

the process
Attach scraps of paper and journaling pieces to a cigar box with spray adhesive. Cover the box with Mod Podge and allow to dry. Sew nickel rectangles to the box to create a closure.

Private Label
BY DEBBIE

Design labels for store-bought soaps, lotions or other bath accessories. Use synonyms and quotations to enhance the labels. Print labels on paper that has been aged with walnut ink. Adhere to bottles. To make the soap covers, cut chipboard to size and score folds. Sew a label to the top. Punch holes in the top and bottom of both sides and lace together with printed twill. Create a patch to stitch onto the cotton bag that houses bath salts. Wrap printed twill around fluffy towels and washcloths. Present the items in a lined basket.

Creativity Junque Book

BY CAROL

the process

Cover an old book with vintage papers. Embellish with a rubber-stamped title, stamped images and other collage items. For the "Thoughts" page, dip a spice bag in walnut ink and allow to dry. Ink the surface of the twill. Let dry. Stamp twill and spice bag with a permanent fabric ink, then heat-set. Insert journaling in the bag. On the opposite page, create a tri-fold card from cardstock. Set eyelets along the sides and weave thin wire in and out. Add a clasp, charms and coin holder. To re-create the "Open Your Eyes" page, brush walnut ink over the page. Cover a rubber-stamped title with mica. Secure the mica with eyelets and wire. For the opposite page, cover white word tiles with vintage-colored alcohol inks. String together with wire and eyelets to create journaling. Add embellishments and stamped words.

Astrology Book
BY KRISTINA

the process

Embellish a journal cover with stamps, stickers, words and other embellishments. Design the inside pages to reflect the theme of the book, such as this astrology book. Include a title page and a few basic information pages. Use various mediums to decorate the pages like paints, papers, stickers, tags, charms, found objects, etc. Once the first page is completed, skip a page to start the next, then go back and adhere the pages together to hide the brads and other embellishments attached to the previous page.

Come Together... Wedding Guest Book

BY JANELLE

the process

Cover and embellish a 7gypsies "gated journal." Print the couple's initials onto mini cards. Have the guests sign a card and slip it into an envelope.

Magnetic Frames *joy*

BY DEBBIE

stylin

Use magnet words to secure photos to the black frame. Cover the other frames with paper. Add words to tiles using Lazertran, following the manufacturer's directions. When transferred, apply a coat of Perfect Paper Adhesive over the top. Glue thin magnets to the backs of the tiles. Glue a piece of decorative stone to the frame with PVA to make a photo ledge.

the process

Altered Clock
BY LISA

the process

Gently remove the hands from a store-bought clock. Create a background by tearing and adhering patterned papers to a piece of heavyweight cardstock using Perfect Paper Adhesive. Place the clock face down onto the background. Trace, then trim. Punch a hole for the clock hands. Apply ephemera and words. Spritz with diluted walnut ink. Shade the edges with brown, green, purple and black ink. Add a final edge of copper. Adhere the completed background to the clock face with Perfect Paper. Reinstall the clock hands.

Friends Wine Charms
BY JENNIFER

the process

Use letter beads to spell "friend" in various languages. String the beads on wire, then hook the wire through holes on folded paper. These wine charms would make great favors at parties or weddings.

chapter twenty

Spread THE word

Do you know the answer to the old joke "What are the three fastest ways to spread the word?" Telephone, telegraph or tell a woman, of course! In this chapter, these women have done their best to spread the word about creative ideas you can use on your next project. Whether you put a chalkboard on your layout, alter a tin or turn your business cards into a mannequin's skirt, the word will soon get around that you're a creative artist!

A Woman of Few Words
BY DEBBIE

the process

Glue printed tissue to body form. Stain several tags with walnut ink. Cut words from the printed tissue to glue to the tags. Add larger tags under the rubber band to make her skirt. Loop mini tags around the push pins to create her shawl. Artist's idea: This would be great to put on a woman's desk to hold creative business cards. The skirt could be made from a person's business cards. Anyone wanting a business card would simply slip one out from the rubber-band waistband.

Home
BY CAROL

This gatefold "house" book is themed around the word "home." For each page, create a collage around a word or group of words containing the word "home." Use stamped images, photos, magazine pages and found objects to decorate the pages.

the process

Chalk Stories
BY CAROL

the process

Sand the covers of a children's board book, then paint with white gesso. Ink with pigment inks. Allow to dry. Brush handmade paper with walnut ink. Wet the paper to remove excess ink, then stamp with alphabet stamps while the paper is wet so the letters appear to "bleed." Allow to dry. Stamp a kraft-colored piece of cardstock with bleach to create the title and by-line. Accent with inks. Add photo to the center. Assemble papers together and create a closure. Stitch lokta string onto paper. Adhere the layered papers to the book covers. For "Tales from the Sidewalk," paint pages with white gesso. Ink with pigment inks and allow to dry. Stamp words using white gesso as the ink. Print a title onto a transparency and adhere to page. To re-create the "Trampoline Art" page, paint pages with white gesso. Ink with pigment inks and allow to dry. Rubber stamp spirals and letters. Add photos. Embellish with brads and wire. Bleach-stamp the title and connect with a spiral easel.

Kindred Spirits
BY JENNIFER

Stamp and print various traits on each side of the ribbon to match the person in the photo.

the process

Kindergarten Checklist
BY RENEE

Paint chipboard with Krylon chalkboard paint. Bind the edges with hinging tape and snap down in each corner. Write the title in chalk, then seal with a fixative.

the process

Make a strong solution of brewed tea. Place paper, ribbon, lace or fabric in a shallow, non-reactive pan. Add tea, then remove the paper immediately. Dry and iron flat with a dry iron. Ribbon, lace and fabric may need to soak for up to an hour for the color to stain the fibers. To create quilted letters, die cut letters from chipboard. Mount letters on tea-stained paper with a paper adhesive. Lay a piece of tea-stained, gauzy fabric over the letters and hand stitch around them.

Wedding
BY CAROL

Altered Tin
BY KRISTINA

Sand the tin lid with sandpaper until the surface is rough. Cover the lid with various papers using Perfect Paper Adhesive. Adhere trinkets, charms, page pebbles, photos, metals, other embellishments and memorabilia. Using stamps and pens, write words to express emotions and events that are contained in the journal and items within the tin. Rubber stamp initials onto a transparency and adhere the piece over vellum. Write on fabric strips with a permanent marker and adhere to the outside rim of the tin.

the process

3 Sisters
BY JANELLE

the process

This journal is for three sisters to share. It has a diary lock holding it closed, and each sister gets a key. The idea is that the journal will be passed from sister to sister. When each sister gets the journal, she must complete a page about an experience or memory she'd like to remember or share, then she passes it to the next sister.

Cover the journal with salmon-colored tissue paper. Let dry, then wash walnut ink over the top. Add photos, found objects and assorted ephemera to the cover. To create the "one," "two" and "three" word frames, adhere the printed words to the back of a nickel rectangle. Fill the frame with PVA. Allow 24 hours to dry and turn clear. Construct a "ledge" from thick cardstock, then embellish with number charms and tags.

in a word

the artists

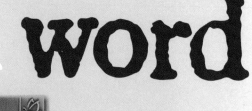

blessed *adj.* **1.** of or enjoying happiness **2.** JENNIFER DITZ MCGUIRE **3.** mechanical engineer turned scrapbook and rubber stamp designer **4.** *Creating Keepsakes* 2002 Hall of Fame inductee **5.** Garden Girl and font designer for Two Peas in a Bucket **6.** published often in many scrapbook magazines **7.** lives in Cincinnati, Ohio **8.** wife to Ken **9.** step "mum" to Kay and Audrey **10.** proud sister of her biggest fan, Mike

sassy *adj.* **1.** impudent, saucy, vigorous, lively, distinctively smart and stylish **2.** RENEE CAMACHO **3.** wife to a wonderfully patient husband, Thomas **4.** mom to three beautiful children – Brandon, Zachary and Kaitlyn **5.** Garden Girl at Two Peas in a Bucket **6.** *Creating Keepsakes* 2002 Hall of Fame inductee **7.** published in several magazines **8.** actively involved in church youth and outreach activities **9.** resides in Nashville, Tennessee

per·snick·e·ty *adj.* **1.** fastidious or attending to detail **2.** DEBBIE CROUSE **3.** contributor to the *Designing With* series **4.** lives in Mesa, Arizona **5.** wife to Skip **6.** mom to four – Jared, Emali, Skyler and Logan **7.** grandma to two and a half **8.** enjoys "thrifting," antiquing, estate sales and general scavenging

ec·lec·tic *adj.* **1.** selecting what appears to be best in various methods or styles **2.** CAROL WINGERT **3.** teaches book arts and scrapbooking workshops at Memory Lane **4.** regularly published in *Legacy* magazine **5.** winner of *Creating Keepsakes* Hall of Fame Honorable Mention in 2002 and 2003 **6.** contributing artist to *Designing with Photos* **7.** just completed her third book for Design Originals **8.** lives in Gilbert, AZ, with husband, Vern, and daughter, Ashley

re·al *adj.* 1. not artificial, fraudulent, illusory, or apparent 2. KRISTINA NICOLAI-WHITE 3. mom to three crazy kids 4. owner of the online scrapbooking community – Two Peas in a Bucket 5. works with her husband, Jeff, and friend, Jamie 6. enjoys meeting hundreds of talented scrapbookers through Two Peas (many of whom she is proud to call friends) 7. lives near Madison, Wisconsin, amid farms, rolling hills and changing seasons

de·vot·ed *adj.* 1. zealous in devotion or affection; "a devoted Mum" 2. TRACY ROBINSON 3. began scrapbooking in April 2001 4. published in *Creating Keepsakes* and *Simple Scrapbooks* 5. proudly part the Two Peas in a Bucket design team 6. a SAHM after a 20-year career in sales & marketing 7. loves her hometown of Melbourne in Australia 8. wife to Graeme and devoted mother to Jemma

pre·cise *adj.* 1. clearly expressed or delineated; definite 2. LISA RUSSO 3. began scrapbooking shortly after the birth of her son in 1999 4. inductee into the 2003 *Creating Keepsakes* Hall of Fame 5. Garden Girl at Two Peas in a Bucket 6. obsessively organizes (and re-organizes) her supplies 7. enjoys reading, photography, exercise and travel 8. lives in Oswego, Illinois, with her husband, Victor, and their four-year-old son, Aidan

gen·u·ine *adj.* 1. free from hypocrisy or pretense 2. JANELLE SMITH 3. earned a fine arts degree in photography from the University of Utah 4. contributor to *Designing with Photos* 5. lives and works as a photographer in Salt Lake City with her husband, Zach, and their son, Zander 6. interests include photography, traveling and spending every spare moment with her ever-curious and energetic 2 1/2 year-old son

product credits

Products without a credit are either part of the artist's personal stash or not available for purchase.

NOTE: All walnut ink is from 7gypsies. And unless otherwise noted, all computer fonts are downloaded from the Internet. 2Peas fonts are downloaded from www.twopeasinabucket.com and CK fonts are from *Creating Keepsakes*.

Chapter 1
Words as Background Noise
Pages 4-9

Blessing
RUBBER STAMPS: Hero Arts, Wordsworth, Ma Vinci's Reliquary, PSX Design, The Missing Link Stamp Company and Limited Edition Rubber Stamps

METALLIC RUB-ONS: Craf-T Products

Climb
PAPER: 7gypsies

COMPUTER FONTS: Butterbrotpapier and 2Peas Bad Attitude

FIBER: FoofaLa

Rugby
PAPER: 7gypsies

SNAPS: Making Memories

BOOKPLATE: Two Peas in a Bucket

COMPUTER FONTS: 1942 Report, Batik Regular, Smash, Chelt Press Trial, Fulton Artistamp, Stamp Act, Harting, 2Peas White Sale, 2Peas Billboard and CK Typewriter

School Book
RUBBER STAMP: Collections

METAL STAMPS: Praiger

PAGE PEBBLE: Making Memories

COMPUTER FONTS: 2Peas Composition, Rough Draft, Rubbermaid and Seraphim

Duets
PAPER: SEI, Bazzill Basics, Chatterbox, Mustard Moon, 7gypsies and KI Memories

VELLUM: Autumn Leaves

CHARMED PHOTO CORNER, EYELETS AND METAL-RIMMED TAGS: Making Memories

RUBBER STAMPS: Ma Vinci's Reliquary, Hero Arts, Stampabilities and PSX Design

Adore Tag
RUBBER STAMPS: Inkadinkado and Hero Arts

POEMSTONE: Sonnets, Creative Imaginations

FIBERS: Rubba Dub Dub, Art Sanctum

OLD MUSIC SHEETS AND PRINTS: www.collagejoy.com

GOLD SPIRAL CLIP: 7gypsies

PAPER: 7gypsies, Sanook Papers and Jennifer Collection

METAL LETTERS: Fancifuls Inc.

Nature
RUBBER STAMPS: Hero Arts and Stampin' Up!

RESIST: Permanent Masking Medium, Winsor & Newton

Wedding Frame
COMPUTER FONTS: 2Peas Flea Market and 2Peas Fiori

PHOTOS: Jana Millen

Studio Bulletin Board
ALPHABET STAMPS: Ma Vinci's Reliquary, Hero Arts, Wordsworth and The Missing Link Stamp Company

BOTTLE, ART RIBBON AND WAXED LINEN: 7gypsies

Wedding Day Bliss
PAPER: Anna Griffin, 7gypsies and Daisy D's

LETTERING TEMPLATE: Wordsworth

RUBBER STAMPS: Hero Arts

PHOTOS: Tammy Batson

Chapter 2
Mark My Word
Pages 10-13

Little Notes
RESIST INK: Ranger Industries

RUBBER STAMPS: Hero Arts

Paris
PAPER: Daisy D's

SLIDE MOUNTS: FoofaLa

MICA TILES: USArtQuest

RUBBER STAMPS: Ma Vinci's Reliquary, JudiKins, PSX Design, Stampa Rosa and Stamp Francisco

Heart
COMPUTER FONT: Splurge

RUBBER STAMPS: Hero Arts, Ma Vinci's Reliquary and Penny Black

Chloe
PAPER: 7gypsies

RUBBER STAMPS: Hero Arts

RIBBON: me and my BIG ideas

Camacho Stationery
PATTERNED PAPER: KI Memories

NICKEL RING: 7gypsies

COMPUTER FONTS: Violation and 2Peas Sailboat

Finicky

TIN: Artistic Impressions

COMPUTER FONTS: Classica and 2Peas Fixin To

GLASS BEADS: JudiKins

RUBBER STAMPS: Hero Arts and Rubber Moon

PHOTO: Jana Millen

Sea and Sand

RUBBER STAMPS: Hero Arts and PSX Design

ALPHABET LETTERS: FoofaLa

VELLUM: Autumn Leaves

A Day in the Park

RUBBER STAMPS: Impress Rubber Stamps, Wordsworth and PSX Design

STITCHED TIN TILES: Making Memories

LABELS: Avery

Chapter 3
Words of Wisdom
Pages 14-17

Fans

COLORLESS BLENDER PEN: Design Art

RUBBER STAMPS: Hero Arts and PSX Design

CORK DISKS: Craft-Rite

CHARMED PHOTO CORNERS: Making Memories

PHOTOS: Cathy Clifford

Sam

RUBBER STAMPS: Hero Arts

PHOTOS: Julie Richardson

Laughter

RUBBER STAMPS: PSX Design, Collections and Hero Arts

BRASS LABEL: Anima Designs

Defining... Comfort

JOURNAL: 7gypsies

FIBERS AND RIBBON: Memory Lane

PAPER: Creative Papers Online

BRADS, ALPHABET CHARM AND PAGE PEBBLE: Making Memories

COMPUTER FONT: CK Typewriter

Wisdom

PAPER AND VELLUM: Treehouse Designs

TICKET STUB AND DICTIONARY PAGE: Manto Fev

DEFINITION, FOOFABETS AND AGING SPONGES: FoofaLa

BOOKPLATE AND TAGS: Two Peas in a Bucket

COMPUTER FONT: 2Peas Chestnuts

GLAZE: Aleene's Paper Glaze

PHOTOS: Tammy Batson

Grow

PAPER: Magenta, 7gypsies and Anna Griffin

NICKEL RECTANGLE: 7gypsies

DEFINITIONS AND ENVELOPE: FoofaLa

COMPUTER FONT: Typist

STICKERS: Nostalgiques

You Card

DEFINITIONS: FoofaLa

COMPUTER FONT: Violation

RUBBER STAMPS: Hero Arts

Chapter 4
The Spoken Word
Pages 18-21

Synchronicity

PAPER: SEI, K & Company and What's New

VELLUM: Autumn Leaves

ALPHABET CHARM AND METAL-RIMMED TAGS: Making Memories

FIBERS: Adornaments

RUBBER STAMPS: Stampers Anonymous, Ma Vinci's Reliquary and Hampton Art Stamps

METAL TYPEWRITER FRAME: Scrapworks

PHOTOS: Danelle Johnson

Words of Wisdom

COMPUTER FONTS: GF Ordner Inverted, GF Ordner Normal, Mom's Typewriter, Valentine, Stamp Act and Tintinabulation

PAPER: Lasting Impressions and 7gypsies

RUBBER STAMPS: Hero Arts and Collections

ACRYLIC GESSO: Liquitex

Book of Psalms

RUBBER STAMPS: Hero Arts

PAPER: 7gypsies and Anna Griffin

SMALL TAGS AND LABEL HOLDER: Two Peas in a Bucket

LIBRARY POCKET: Manto Fev

Get Married!

COMPUTER FONTS: Classic Typewriter and Blackjack

PAPER: Colors by Design and K & Company

BRASS FRAME: Nunn Design

BOOK PLATE: Two Peas in a Bucket

BRASS PHOTO CORNERS: 7gypsies

CANVAS CLOTH PAPER: Office Depot

SNAPS: Making Memories

The Beauty of the Seasons

TRANSFER PAPER: Epson

COMPUTER FONTS: John Handy LET and Teletype

PHOTOS: Jane Gibbons-Eyre

Excerpts

COMPUTER FONT: John Doe

SNAPS: Making Memories

ELASTIC: 7gypsies

BOOKPLATE: Two Peas in a Bucket

RUBBER STAMPS: The Moon Rose and Stampers Anonymous

Tile Coasters

COMPUTER FONTS: 2Peas Prose, 2Peas Blissful and 2Peas Sailboat

INKS: Studio II

Chapter 5
Drop a Line
Pages 22-25

Me, Defined

TAGS: FoofaLa

RUBBER STAMPS: PSX Design and Hero Arts

NETTING: Magic Scraps

STAMPS AND MICA:
Manto Fev

PAGE PEBBLES:
Making Memories

VELLUM ENVELOPE:
Impress Rubber Stamps

LINEN HINGING TAPE:
Lineco

The Family She Left Behind

COMPUTER FONTS:
Dominican and Carpenter

PAPER: 7gypsies and
K & Company

SNAPS: Making Memories

RUBBER STAMPS: Hero Arts,
Hampton Art Stamps, PSX
Design, Stampers Anonymous
and Inkadinkado

EXTREME EYELETS:
Creative Imaginations

RIBBON: Memory Lane

CLOCK FACE: Manto Fev

Vintage Envelope Card

PAPER: 7gypsies

FRAME: Nunn Design

RIBBON: Memory Lane

RUBBER STAMP: A Stamp
in the Hand

Secrets

RUBBER STAMPS: Hero
Arts, Stamp Oasis, Stampers
Anonymous, PSX Design, The
Missing Link Stamp Company
and Stampa Rosa

COMPUTER FONTS:
2Peas Ragtag, 2Peas Billboard
and Migraine Serif

Photo Postage Cards

PAPER: Daisy D's

COMPUTER FONTS: 2Peas
Lighthouse, 2Peas Submarine,
Chelt Press and Blackjack

Chapter 6
Play on Words
Pages 26-29

Brandon

RUBBER STAMPS: PSX Design

**BINGO CARDS, STAMPS AND
SLIDE MOUNTS:** Manto Fev

NAILHEADS: Two Peas in
a Bucket

Crossword

COMPUTER FONT:
Typewriter, P22

PAPER: K & Company

**TAGS, EYELET, SNAPS AND
CHARMED FRAME:** Making
Memories

**COMPASS CHARM AND
TYPEWRITER-KEY FRAME:**
Two Peas in a Bucket

RUBBER STAMPS: Hero Arts

Play

PAPER: SEI, KI Memories,
Bazzill Basics and K & Company

VELLUM: Autumn Leaves

RUBBER STAMPS:
Ma Vinci's Reliquary, Hero Arts
and PSX Design

**ALPHABET CHARMS AND
CHARMED PHOTO CORNER:**
Making Memories

LETTER STICKERS: Sonnets,
Creative Imaginations

Artist

COMPUTER FONTS:
Chelt Press Trial and Smash

CLOCK FINDING: 7gypsies

METAL-RIMMED TAG AND

SNAPS: Making Memories

RUBBER STAMPS: Limited
Edition Rubber Stamps and
Stampers Anonymous

PHOTOS: Cathy Zielske

Your Wish is My Command

STAMPS: Manto Fev

PAPER: Design Originals
and 7gypsies

Seeds Shaker Box Accordion Book

RUBBER STAMPS: Stamp
Camp and Paper Inspirations

CHARM: Fancifuls Inc.

DRIED FLOWER: Colorbök

Play Hard

PAPERS: Design Originals
and KI Memories

RUBBER STAMPS: Hero Arts

TICKET STUBS: Manto Fev

BRADS: Lost Art Treasures

COMPUTER FONTS: 2Peas
Sailboat, 2Peas Submarine,
2Peas Essential, 2Peas Katherine
Ann, Rockwell, Violation,
Decker and 39 Smooth

PHOTOS: Tammy Batson

Connect Four

GAME PIECES: Connect Four,
Milton Bradley

COIN HOLDER: Hobby Lobby

COMPUTER FONTS: 2Peas
Yo-Yo, 2Peas Submarine, 2Peas
Lighthouse, Annifont, Four
Decibels and Falling

RIVETS: Chatterbox

RUBBER STAMPS: Hero Arts

PHOTOS: Jana Millen, Sherri
Marshall and Lara Williams

Travel Journal

ACCORDION-BOOK KIT:
Books By Hand

CLASP: 7gypsies

COMPASS AND HEMP:
Memory Lane

JOURNEY BRASS PLATE:
Ink It!

**GIRAFFE AND VINTAGE
MAP:** www.collagejoy.com

Chapter 7
Softly Spoken
Pages 30-31

New

COMPUTER FONT:
Cezanne, P22

**PAPER, BOX CLOSURE AND
SILVER RING:** 7gypsies

SILVER FRAME: Nunn Design

Winter Angel

COMPUTER FONT: Barbara

RUBBER STAMPS: Hero Arts
and Impress Rubber Stamps

Laugh

PAPER: SEI, KI Memories
and Doodlebug

VELLUM: Autumn Leaves

RUBBER STAMPS: Ma Vinci's
Reliquary, Junque and The
Missing Link Stamp Company

ALPHABET PAGE PEBBLES:
Making Memories

Thoughts... Fantasies

PAPER: Anna Griffin

LETTER TEMPLATES:
Wordsworth and American
Traditional Stencils

CLAY SHARD: Alicia G.

COMPUTER FONT:
CK Cursive

Chapter 8
Words that Make an Impact
Pages 32-35

Quirky
ALPHABET STICKERS: Nostalgiques
PAPER: SEI

Fate: An Anniversary Card
COMPUTER FONTS: Typewriter and Rodin, P22; Stamp Act
EXTREME EYELET: Creative Imaginations
CHARMS: Two Peas in a Bucket and 7gypsies
RUBBER STAMPS: JudiKins, Stampabilities, Hero Arts, Inkadinkado, Penny Black, Stampington & Co. and Stampers Anonymous

Frolic
PAINT: Lumiere, Jacquard Products
ACRYLIC GESSO: Liquitex
ALPHABET STAMPS: Wordsworth
RUBBER STAMPS: Hero Arts
SNAPS: Making Memories

Sculpture
PAPER: Sonnets, KI Memories, 7gypsies and SEI
VELLUM: Autumn Leaves
RUBBER STAMPS: Ma Vinci's Reliquary
CHARMED PHOTO CORNER: Making Memories

Hilarious Frame
PAPER: Design Originals and 7gypsies
RUBBER STAMPS: PSX Design

Electric Blue
ELECTRICAL COMPONENTS: www.collagejoy.com
COIN HOLDERS: Hobby Lobby
ALPHABET STAMPS: Hero Arts
COMPUTER FONT: Mostolios

Reflection
PARCHMENT: Ink It!
HANDMADE PAPER: Hollanders
NAILHEADS AND SPIRALE: 7gypsies
MIRROR TILES: ARTchix Studio
STICKER LETTERS: Stampendous
PAINT: Lumiere, Jacquard Products

Dauntless
BUCKLES: Dritz
BUTTONS: Hero Arts
RUBBER STAMPS: Magenta, Hero Arts and Stamp Oasis

Chapter 9
In Your Own Words
Pages 36-37

Walk with Angels
PAPER: KI Memories and 7gypsies
FRAME: Hap's Memories
FRAME HOOKS: Hobby Lobby
VELLUM: Autumn Leaves

Supergirl
PAPER: SEI, KI Memories, Paper Fever and Doodlebug
VELLUM: Autumn Leaves
RUBBER STAMPS: Hero Arts
ALPHABET CHARMS AND METAL-RIMMED TAG: Making Memories
LETTER STICKERS: Mrs. Grossman's

2003: Year in Review
LARGE SNAP ENVELOPE: Paper Source
RUSTY HEART: Provo Craft
PAPER: K & Company, Sonnets, Mustard Moon, Sarah Lugg and Karen Foster Design
VELLUM: Chatterbox
RUBBER STAMPS: Hampton Art Stamps, Stampers Anonymous and PSX Design
METAL-RIMMED TAG, CHARMED PHOTO CORNERS AND EYELET CHARM: Making Memories
CLOCK FACE: 7gypsies

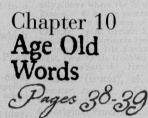

Chapter 10
Age Old Words
Pages 38-39

Through the Eyes of a Child
TRANSFER PAPER: Lazertran
RUBBER STAMPS: Ma Vinci's Reliquary, Uptown Design, Stampland and JudiKins
STENCIL: Wordsworth
LABEL: FoofaLa
COPPER HEART: Ink It!
HEART BUTTON: La Mode
BENDABLE METAL HEART: Stampington & Co.

Three Sisters
COMPUTER FONTS: Teletype and Sloop Script Two
STITCHED TIN TILE: Making Memories
GOLD BAR: 7gypsies
HEART BEAD: Bazaar Beads
CHARM AND GOLD FRAME: Two Peas in a Bucket
PAPER: K & Company and Autumn Leaves

Secrets
PAPER: Paper Stuff
PRINTED TWILL TAPE: 7gypsies
DOMINOS, RIBBON AND WAXED COTTON: Memory Lane
TYPEWRITER LETTERS: Nostalgiques

Grow in Beauty
PAPER: Anna Griffin and 7gypsies
OVAL WOOD PIECE: Manto Fev
WOOD STRIP: Michaels
WOOD-BURNING TOOL: Walnut Hollow

Chapter 11
Spoken Clearly
Pages 40-45

Pout
PAPER: K & Company
MICA CHIPS: Paper Moon
COMPUTER FONT: 2Peas Chestnuts
RUBBER STAMPS: PSX Design and Hero Arts
LABELS: FoofaLa
GLAZE: Aleene's Paper Glaze

Worry

ALPHABET STAMPS:
Hero Arts and Hampton
Art Stamps

PAPER: 7gypsies and
Memory Lane

SPIRALE: 7gypsies

LEAFING: Amy's Leafing Magic

Cards

RUBBER STAMPS:
Close to My Heart, Stampin'
Up!, Hero Arts and Impress
Rubber Stamps

COMPUTER FONTS:
Grammes and Texas Hero

Family

PAPER: Design Originals and
7gypsies

**LETTER STICKERS AND
RUB-ONS:** Creative
Imaginations

RIVETS: Chatterbox

COMPUTER FONTS: Xerox
Sans Serif Wide, Zapfino
Linotype One, Violation,
2Peas Submarine and
Perspective Sans Black

You Belong to Me

PAPER: SEI, Chatterbox,
Sonnets, Doodlebug and
7gypsies

VELLUM: Autumn Leaves

**EYELETS AND METAL-
RIMMED TAG:** Making
Memories

RUBBER STAMPS: Ma Vinci's
Reliquary and Hero Arts

Angelic

PAPER: K & Company
and Sanook

RUBBER STAMPS: PSX
Design and Hero Arts

PHOTOS: Leslie Lightfoot

Prayer Journal

PAPER: Treehouse Designs,
Anna Griffin and 7gypsies

**DEFINITIONS AND
FLEXIBLE MICROSCOPE
SLIDES:** FoofaLa

EYELETS AND WIRE:
Making Memories

JOURNAL AND RIBBON:
7gypsies

Timeless

PAPER: SEI, KI Memories
and Sonnets

VELLUM: Autumn Leaves

METAL-RIMMED TAG:
Making Memories

RUBBER STAMPS:
Stampendous, Ma Vinci's
Reliquary and Stampers
Anonymous

Tender

1/8" PLASTIC: Hobby Lobby

COMPUTER FONT: 2Peas
Yo-Yo

FROSTED GLASS FINISH:
Krylon

**GOLD- AND COPPER-
LEAFING PEN:** Krylon

RUBBER STAMPS: Hero Arts

Art Journal

WOODEN BOOK:
Walnut Hollow

WOODEN LETTERS:
Provo Craft

METAL VINE: Westrim

STAMP PAPER:
Stampington & Co.

LEAVES: Black Ink

RUBBER STAMP:
Stampers Anonymous

PAINT: Lumiere, Jacquard
Products

WAX: Yaley Enterprises

Mica Cards

STICKERS: Nostalgiques

RUBBER STAMPS: Hero Arts
and PSX Design

**CLOCK FINDINGS AND
NAILHEAD:** 7gypsies

SQUARE NAILHEAD:
Scrapworks

EYELET WORD:
Making Memories

PAPER: Anna Griffin

Clear Bookmarks

COMPUTER FONTS:
Franklin Gothic, Still Time and
Franklin Gothic Book

SILVER LEAFING: Mona Lisa
Products, Houston Art, Inc.

GLUE PEN: Zig

Chapter 12
Words from the Printing Press
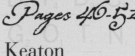
Pages 46-51

Keaton

COMPUTER FONT:
CK Template

BOOK PLATE:
Anima Designs

PHOTOS: Allison Tyler Jones

Memory Journal

COMPUTER FONTS:
Typewriter and Rodin, P22;
Stamp Act and Hootie

RUBBER STAMPS: Stampers
Anonymous, The Missing
Link Stamp Company, Hero
Arts, Uptown Rubber Stamps,
Renaissance Art Stamps and A
Stamp in the Hand

STICKERS: Nostalgiques and
Creative Imaginations

**BOOKPLATE & NICKEL
MINI BRADS:** Two Peas in a
Bucket

**NICKEL SQUARE, NICKEL
RINGS, DOUBLE SPIRALE
AND WATCH FACE:**
7gypsies

MAGIC MESH: Avant Card

WATCH CRYSTAL:
Memory Lane

Friends

COMPUTER FONTS:
Typewriter, P22; Chelt
Press Trial

PAPER: 7gypsies

METAL-RIMMED TAGS:
Making Memories

Determination

WIRE MESH: Home Depot

**METAL-RIMMED TAG, RUB-
ONS AND DEFINED
STICKERS:** Making Memories

Peace and Sleep

PAPER: K & Company
and 7gypsies

RUBBER STAMPS: Hero Arts
and Hampton Art Stamps

COMPUTER FONTS:
Carpenter and Harting

NICKEL SPINE: 7gypsies

PHOTOS: Marilyn Healey

Notes from Grandma

RUBBER STAMPS: Hero Arts

COMPUTER FONTS:
Garamouche, P22; Pablo

Strum

COMPUTER FONTS:
Stencil and Texas Hero

Dreams

BRAD: 7gypsies

PHOTOS: Jane Gibbons-Eyre

100% Authentic

PAPER: Daisy D's

NAILHEADS: 7gypsies

Bag It!

**KEY CHARM, FRAME
CHARM AND MESSAGE
BOTTLE:** 7gypsies

Chapter 13
Words to Impress
Pages 52-53

Nature Folio
CRAFTING COPPER: Amaco

RUBBER STAMPS: Ma Vinci's Reliquary, A Stamp in the Hand, Stamp Zia and Stampers Anonymous

SILVER LEAFING PEN: Krylon

WAXY FLAX: Scrapworks

Hope
RUBBER STAMPS: Hero Arts and PSX Design

PAPER: Anna Griffin, Creative Imaginations, 7gypsies and Daisy D's

DEFINITION: FoofaLa

Backyard Paradise
FAUX LEATHER: Comotion

RUBBER STAMPS: Ma Vinci's Reliquary and Hero Arts

METALLIC RUB-ONS: Craf-T Products

PAPER: Creative Imaginations and Memory Lane

METAL LETTERS: Making Memories

TICKET STUBS AND FLOWER SEED PACKET: www.collagejoy.com

Chapter 14
Repeat After Me
Pages 54-57

Time
PAPER: Chatterbox

STITCHED TIN TILES: Making Memories

COMPUTER FONTS: Texas Hero and Sylfaen

RUBBER STAMPS: Hero Arts, Collections Australia, JudiKins and Impress Rubber Stamps

Embrace
PAPER: 7gypsies and KI Memories

WAXED LINEN, WATCH PARTS AND BEAD BOTTLE: 7gypsies

STICKERS: Stickopotamus

RUBBER STAMPS: Hero Arts

SNAPS: Chatterbox

COMPUTER FONTS: Caeldera, Elastic Wrath and Amano

TRANSFER PAPER AND FABRIC: Daisy Kingdom

SHAPED CLIP: Making Memories

PHOTO: Melissa Olsen

Art Journal
RUBBER STAMPS: Hero Arts and Collections Australia

TRANSFER PAPER: Epson

COMPUTER FONT: Seraphim

Serenity
PATTERNED PAPER: 7gypsies

STICKERS: Sonnets, Creative Imaginations

ALPHABET CHARMS: Making Memories

LETTER BEADS: Hobby Lobby

TWILL TAPE AND ELASTICS: 7gypsies

ALPHABET STAMPS: Hero Arts

CLEAR BOOKPLATE: KI Memories

PHOTO: Jana Millen

Dream
PAPER: SEI, Sonnets, 7gypsies and Doodlebug

VELLUM: Autumn Leaves

RUBBER STAMPS: Ma Vinci's Reliquary and Stampers Anonymous

ALPHABET CHARMS, PAGE PEBBLE AND METAL-RIMMED TAG: Making Memories

LETTER STICKERS: Sonnets, Creative Imaginations; Mrs. Grossmans

METAL WORD: Sonnets, Creative Imaginations

Love
RUBBER STAMPS: Hero Arts

WAXED LINEN: 7gypsies

Chapter 15
Signed, Sealed and Delivered
Pages 58-59

Dearest Karen
POEMSTONES: Sonnets, Creative Imaginations

COMPUTER FONT: Willing Race

PAPER: Daisy D's

RUBBER STAMPS: Hero Arts and The Missing Link Stamp Company

Snips and Snails
PAPER: SEI, K & Company and Sonnets

RUBBER STAMPS: PSX Design

METAL-RIMMED TAG: Making Memories

BRADS: American Tag

COMPUTER FONTS: 2Peas Jack Frost and 2Peas Chestnuts

RIBBON END CLIPS: Scrapworks

ENVELOPE: Paper Source

Inside Out
CANVAS PAPER: Strathmore

PATTERNED PAPER: 7gypsies

Graduation Tin
CYLINDRICAL TIN AND RIBBON: Memory Lane

PAPER: 7gypsies and Memory Lane

WATCH FACE: Manto Fev

ELASTIC, WAXED LINEN AND SILVER STUDS: 7gypsies

RUBBER STAMPS: Green Pepper Press, PSX Design, Stampa Rosa, Rubber Stampede and Hero Arts

Chapter 16
Calling Cards
Pages 60-61

ZKB
PAPER: KI Memories

RUBBER STAMPS: Hero Arts

GLASSINE ENVELOPE: Memory Lane

AW
PAPER: SEI, K & Company, Doodlebug and KI Memories

VELLUM: Autumn Leaves

SHAPED CLIP, ALPHABET CHARM, EYELET LETTERS AND SQUARE BRADS: Making Memories

COMPUTER FONTS: 2Peas Jack Frost and 2Peas Chestnuts

NICKEL RING: 7gypsies

HEART CHARM: Magenta

i get to hear my children

Monogram Tag

PAPER: Memory Lane and Ink It!

WOODEN LETTER: Walnut Hollow

GLASS BOTTLE: ARTchix Studio

LOKTA STRING: Creative Papers Online

PAINT: Lumiere, Jacquard Products

It's All About Me

BUTTONS: Dress It Up

RIBBON: 7gypsies and May Arts

SAFETY PINS: Dritz

JMA

PAPER: K & Company, 7gypsies and Magenta

WIRE: Making Memories

COMPUTER FONTS: Blackjack and 2Peas Prose

METALLIC RUB-ONS: Craf-T Products

Chapter 17
Song Lyrics
Pages 62-63

Remember When

SONG LYRICS: Addy-Ram

TRANSFER PAPER: Lazertran

ENAMEL PLATE: 7gypsies

ALCOHOL INKS: Studio II

Life Card

COMPUTER FONT: Leftovers

SONG LYRICS: Bee Gees

I Have Been Blessed

JOURNAL: 7gypsies

BOOK CORNERS, WALNUT-INKED TAG AND WAXED LINEN: 7gypsies

METAL TAGS: DieCuts with a View

BRAD LETTERS, LETTER STICKERS AND PUZZLE STICKERS: Creative Imaginations

COMPUTER FONTS: Fontdinerdotcom, Lumos, Roughage, Ashley and Gutter

SQUARE CARDS: KI Memories

VINTAGE LABELS: FoofaLa

Lighthouse

COMPUTER FONT: Fountain Pen Frenzy

LOVE DISC: 7gypsies

RUBBER STAMPS: Collections Australia

White Family Music Journal

JOURNAL: 7gypsies

PAPER: KI Memories, Pamela Woods, Paper Fever, Sweetwater, Chatterbox, Bazzill Basics and Sonnets

ALPHABET CHARM: Making Memories

LETTER STICKERS: Sonnets, Doodlebug, SEI, me and my BIG ideas, Wordsworth, Provo Craft, EK Success and Creative Imaginations

Chapter 18
Word on the Street
Pages 64-65

Marquee Cards

ALPHABET STAMPS: The Missing Link Stamp Company and Turtle Press

Fresh and New

PAPER AND ACCENT BLOCKS: KI Memories

COMPUTER FONTS: Haettenschweiler, Street Bold and Rockwell

Signs of Our Daily Life

COMPUTER FONTS: Hammerkeys and LainieDaySH

5 Days in Portland

PAPER: 7gypsies, SEI and Frances Meyer

TINKER PINS AND CAPSULE: 7gypsies

PAGE PEBBLES: Making Memories

COMPUTER FONTS: 1942 Report, Lumos, Mandingo, Miserable and Amano; Cezanne, P22

RUBBER STAMPS: Hero Arts

Chapter 19
The Gift of Words
Pages 66-71

Light Tomorrow

CANDLES AND TRAY: Cost Plus World Market

CHARM: Two Peas in a Bucket

COMPUTER FONT: 2Peas Lighthouse

RUBBER STAMPS: Hero Arts

Live the Life

NICKEL RECTANGLES AND TWILL RIBBON: 7gypsies

PAPER: 7gypsies, Anna Griffin, me and my BIG ideas and Autumn Leaves

ORCHESTRA TICKET: me and my BIG ideas

COMPUTER FONTS: Hannibal Lecter, JJ Stencil Trial Version and Rudelsberg

Private Label

COMPUTER FONT: Arts and Crafts, P22; Linen Stroke and Hootie

TWILL AND MUSLIN BAGS: 7gypsies

TOILETRIES AND CANDLES: Bath and Body Works and Votivo

Creativity Junque Book

CLASP: 7gypsies

BUTTERFLY CHARMS: Nunn Design

COIN HOLDER: Memory Lane

RUBBER STAMPS: Green Pepper Press, Stampers Anonymous, Stamp Camp, JudiKins and Stampa Rosa

COMPUTER FONT: CK Typewriter

PAPER: Anna Griffin, K & Company and Memory Lane

BOOK PLATE: Anima Designs

CHARMS AND WORD TILES: Stampers Anonymous

POSTCARD AND BRASS FRAME: Ink It!

OPTIC LENS: ARTchix Studio

MICA TILE: USArtQuest

Astrology Book

LETTER STICKERS: Sonnets, Doodlebug, Wordsworth, EK Success, Creative Imaginations, Mrs. Grossman's, SEI and Making Memories

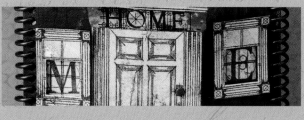

METALS AND HARDWARE: Making Memories, 7gypsies and Scrapworks

PAPER: Mustard Moon, KI Memories, Creative Imaginations, 7gypsies, Karen Foster Design, Inspire2, Autumn Leaves, Sonnets, SEI, Frances Meyer, Paper Fever, Jennifer Collection, Doodlebug and Chatterbox

RUBBER STAMPS: Hero Arts, Hampton Art Stamps, Stampers Anonymous, Ma Vinci's Reliquary, Beeswax, Uptown Rubber Stamps and PSX Design

Come Together... Wedding Guest Book

JOURNAL, PAPER AND FRENCH ENAMEL: 7gypsies

EYELET PHRASES AND EYELET LETTERS: Making Memories

COMPUTER FONTS: Mandingo, Caeldera and Amano; Cezanne, P22

RIBBON: Daisy Kingdom

RUBBER STAMPS: Hero Arts

Magnetic Frames

PAPER: 7gypsies

COMPUTER FONTS: Gilde, Hootie and John Doe

MAGNETIC WORDS: Magnetic Poetry, Inc.

TRANSFER PAPER: Lazertran

Altered Clock

PATTERNED PAPERS: Mustard Moon, K & Company, Design Originals and Rusty Pickle

STICKERS AND EPHEMERA: me and my BIG ideas and Paper Reflections

LETTER STICKERS: Sonnets, Creative Imaginations; Nostalgiques, SEI and me and my BIG ideas

SCRABBLE LETTERS: Limited Edition Rubber Stamps

FOOFABET LETTERS: FoofaLa

PAGE PEBBLE LETTERS, EYELET NUMBERS AND ALPHABET CHARMS: Making Memories

BOOKPLATE: Two Peas in a Bucket

BRASS CLAMPS AND CLEAR ROUND FRAMES: Scrapworks

RUBBER STAMPS: Hero Arts, Limited Edition Rubber Stamps and Plaid Enterprises

CLOCK NAILHEAD AND WATCH FACE: 7gypsies

METALLIC RUB-ONS: Craf-T Products

Friends Wine Charm

LETTER BEADS AND RINGS: Hobby Lobby

COMPUTER FONT: Patchanka

PAPER: KI Memories

TRANSLATIONS INTO OTHER LANGUAGES: www.freetranslation.com

Chapter 20
Spread the Word
Pages 72-75

A Woman of Few Words

DRESS FORM: Michaels

TISSUE PAPER, TAGS AND RUBBER BAND: 7gypsies

Home

GATEFOLD-BOOK KIT: Green Pepper Press

RUBBER STAMPS: Hampton Art Stamps, Postmodern Design, Green Pepper Press and VIP Arts

PAINT: Neopaque, Jacquard Products

WALNUT-INKED TAGS: 7gypsies

COPPER: Amaco

PATINA FINISHING SOLUTION: Chemtek

FILM STRIPS AND TICKET: www.collagejoy.com

Chalk Stories

PAPER: Memory Lane and Ink It!

ACRYLIC GESSO: Liquitex

RUBBER STAMPS: Stampers Anonymous, The Missing Link Stamp Company, Postmodern Design, Embossing Arts Co. and Ma Vinci's Reliquary

LOKTA STRING: Creative Papers Online

ENVELOPE: FoofaLa

ALPHABET CHARM: Making Memories

EASEL SPIRALE: 7gypsies

PHOTOS: Allison Tyler Jones

Kindred Spirits

RUBBER STAMPS: Hero Arts

CALLIGRAPHY NIBS: www.collagejoy.com

HEARTS: KI Memories

WHITE AND BLACK LETTERS: from KI Memories paper

ALPHABET CHARMS: Making Memories

FAUX TYPEWRITER KEYS: Limited Edition Rubber Stamps

PHOTO: Jana Millen

Kindergarten Checklist

PAPER: Sonnets, Creative Imaginations

SNAPS: Making Memories

EPHEMERA: Manto Fev

LINEN HINGING TAPE: Lineco

CHALKBOARD PAINT: Krylon

Wedding

PATTERNED PAPER: K & Company

TINY FLOWER: Creative Papers Online

Altered Tin

LETTER STICKERS: Sonnets and Doodlebug

PAPER: Sonnets, KI Memories, Chatterbox and 7gypsies

METAL FRAME AND ALPHABET CHARMS: Making Memories

RUBBER STAMPS: Ma Vinci's Reliquary and Stampers Anonymous

3 Sisters

PHOTOS: Melissa Olsen

JOURNAL: 7gypsies

PAPER: 7gypsies, SEI and Frances Meyer

SCRAPBOOK NAILS: Chatterbox

MINI BUTTONS: Jest Charming Embellishments

METAL NUMBERS: Making Memories

WAXED LINEN, DIVINE TYPE KEY, ELASTIC AND METAL RECTANGLES: 7gypsies

FLOWERS: Jolee's Boutique

COMPUTER FONT: Mandingo

RUBBER STAMPS: Hero Arts

about us

Autumn Leaves began in the stationery industry over six years ago. At one point, we noticed that paper sales were increasing at a far greater pace than envelope sales. After a time, we discovered that our papers were being purchased by scrapbookers who, of course, didn't need envelopes; just beautiful papers. 'Lo and behold, a new company was born!

Soon after, Autumn leaves began making stickers and vellum pages, becoming well-known for layered, lush vellums and the acquisition of the popular Whispers line of photographic vellums.

Realizing the need for an idea book about vellum, Autumn Leaves published *Designing with Vellum* in September 2001 and launched its publishing division. *Designing with Notions* was next in the series, followed by *Designing with Texture*.

This has been an eventful year for us. It started off with the incredibly successful introduction of the 7gypsies line of embellishments, papers and albums, designed for Autumn Leaves.

Summertime brought the release of the tremendously popular *Designing with Photos*. Through it all, we've managed to stay ahead of the trends, leading the industry with the best and brightest artists the scrapbooking world has to offer.

The book you hold in your hands is no exception. Jennifer Ditz McGuire and Renee Camacho lead a group of eight talented artists from across the spectrum of scrapbooking and paper arts to bring you *Designing with Words*. This eclectic group presents techniques from book arts to rubber stamping; collage to scrapbooking with a few stops in-between for Debbie Crouse's signature pieces.

As our little collection of books has grown it has affectionately been dubbed the DW series. Enjoy your copy of DWW, *Designing with Words* that is, and keep an eye out for much more in the DW series, coming to a store near you.

Autumn Leaves

A full line of papers, vellums, books, and stickers, and adding exciting new categories each year!

Stickers

National Cardstock

America's Fastest Growing Cardstock Company

7gypsies
www.sevengypsies.com
For Autumn Leaves

collections from the journey

Gypsy Jewelry

Autumn Leaves
4917 Genesta St.
Encino, CA. 91316

For Information, Contact:

Josie Kinnear .[Operations Manager]
Alanna Arthur ...[Projects Manager]
Tim Collins .... [Marketing Director]

Vellums

Papers

Journals

Papers

Long Distance
1.800.588.6707

Local
1.818.907.5977

Fax
1.818.380.6776

To Contact National Cardstock Please Call:
P. 1.866.452.7120 | F. 1.866.452.7121

tired

adj. **1.** drained of strength and energy, fatigued often to the point of exhaustion

One word to describe us all:

During the production of this book, we found ourselves busier than ever. Here's a behind-the-scenes look at what has made us all tired. Lisa sold and bought a house, moving from Georgia to Illinois. Debbie had a son graduate from high school, worked with her church's young women's group, and was involved in a youth dance festival, all the while working and designing for 7gypsies. Tracy juggled a busy life being a mother to Jemma and a wife to Graeme along with finding creative time. Renee had a summer full of youth activities (car washes, fundraisers, day trips and rallies), church activities and three children all home for the summer. Carol had a daughter graduate from high school, ran a business in partnership with her husband, and taught classes at Memory Lane, her LSS. Jennifer got married, became a step-mom, moved *and* had a job change. Kristina 'mommied' her three young children and worked about 50 hours a week. Janelle was in school full time and opened her own photography studio. She also completely remodeled and moved into a new home. And the writer, Erin, sold and bought a house and had a baby (writing the majority of this book four days after giving birth — we are all still amazed at this!)

Despite being busy and tired, we have managed to find the time for creativity, time to do the things we all love! We hope you'll take time out of your hectic schedule to be creative and express your *feelings with words* on your works of art.